Timeless Paganism

Ancient Traditions, Modern Mysteries - An In-Depth Exploration of Norse Magic, Celtic Rhythms, and Other Pagan Practices

© Copyright 2024- All rights reserved.

The content contained within this book may not be reproduced, duplicated, or transmitted without direct written permission from the author or the publisher.

Under no circumstances will any blame or legal responsibility be held against the publisher, or author, for any damages, reparation, or monetary loss due to the information contained within this book, either directly or indirectly.

Legal Notice:

This book is copyright protected. It is only for personal use. You cannot amend, distribute, sell, use, quote, or paraphrase any part, or the content within this book, without the consent of the author or publisher.

Disclaimer Notice:

Please note the information contained within this document is for educational and entertainment purposes only. All effort has been executed to present accurate, up-to-date, reliable, and complete information. No warranties of any kind are declared or implied. Readers acknowledge that the author is not engaging in the rendering of legal, financial, medical, or professional advice. The content within this book has been derived from various sources. Please consult a licensed professional before attempting any techniques outlined in this book.

By reading this document, the reader agrees that under no circumstances is the author responsible for any losses, direct or indirect, that are incurred as a result of the use of the information contained within this document, including, but not limited to, errors, omissions, or inaccuracies.

Your Free Gift
(only available for a limited time)

Thanks for getting this book! If you want to learn more about various spirituality topics, then join Mari Silva's community and get a free guided meditation MP3 for awakening your third eye. This guided meditation mp3 is designed to open and strengthen ones third eye so you can experience a higher state of consciousness. Simply visit the link below the image to get started.

https://spiritualityspot.com/meditation

Or, Scan the QR code!

Table of Contents

PART 1: PAGANISM FOR BEGINNERS 1
   INTRODUCTION 2
   CHAPTER 1: WHAT IS PAGANISM? 4
   CHAPTER 2: CELTIC PAGANISM AND DRUIDRY 15
   CHAPTER 3: ASATRU: NORSE PAGANISM 26
   CHAPTER 4: GERMANIC PAGANISM 39
   CHAPTER 5: SLAVIC PAGANISM 50
   CHAPTER 6: GREEK POLYTHEISM 61
   CHAPTER 7: WICCA: A NEOPAGAN VIEW 72
   CHAPTER 8: APPLYING YOUR PAGAN BELIEFS TO DAILY LIFE 83
   APPENDIX: A-Z OF THE WHEEL OF THE YEAR 93
   CONCLUSION 100
PART 2: NORSE PAGANISM 102
   INTRODUCTION 103
   CHAPTER 1: PAGANISM 101 105
   CHAPTER 2: NORSE RELIGION: OLD AND MODERN 115
   CHAPTER 3: THE ASATRU RELIGION 126
   CHAPTER 4: THE SOUL AND THE AFTERLIFE 136
   CHAPTER 5: FYLGJA: FINDING YOUR GUARDIAN 144
   CHAPTER 6: THE MAGIC OF SEIDR 155
   CHAPTER 7: UTESITTA: SITTING OUT, SEEKING WITHIN 164
   CHAPTER 8: RUNIC MAGIC AND DIVINATION 173
   CHAPTER 9: BINDRUNES AND SIGILS 183

CHAPTER 10: STADHAGALDR: RUNIC YOGA 191
GLOSSARY OF TERMS 200
CONCLUSION 205
HERE'S ANOTHER BOOK BY MARI SILVA THAT YOU MIGHT LIKE 207
YOUR FREE GIFT (ONLY AVAILABLE FOR A LIMITED TIME) 208
REFERENCES 209
IMAGE SOURCES 220

Part 1: Paganism for Beginners

An Essential Guide to Celtic, Norse, Slavic, Germanic, and Greek Pagan Practices and the Wheel of the Year

Introduction

What is Paganism? Is it an ancient religion or a modern practice? Does it still exist, and if so, what does it look like today? These are some questions asked about Paganism as interest in this long-standing tradition grows. Many are drawn to the idea of honoring nature and paying homage to deities generally forgotten by modern society. Yet with diverse cultures coming together to share their knowledge in the 21st century, it can be difficult to pinpoint what makes up pagan traditions.

From Wicca to Asatru and other practices which have influenced the world today, each has its beliefs making up its unique framework. Exploring Paganism brings many opportunities for self-reflection and understanding ancient cultures and modern practices, which continue to fascinate scholars everywhere. This book will help you explore the history and practice of these religions, demystifying them and providing practical advice to use Paganism in your everyday life.

Paganism is an umbrella term encompassing a wide variety of spiritual beliefs and practices, from Wicca and Druidry to Asatru and Pantheism. These faiths draw upon nature-based traditions that have been practiced since before recorded history. Each has unique rituals, symbols, practices, and ways of living harmoniously with the natural world.

This book provides an easy-to-understand overview of the various forms of Paganism so you can make a more informed decision about the right path for you. No matter what your knowledge level or experience with these practices, this book will give you everything to get started on your personal journey into Paganism. From understanding the core concepts and discovering their roots in human history to exploring rituals performed by neopagans, this book is a one-stop solution to Paganism.

This enlightening book delves deep into various pagan cultures, providing an intriguing look into each perspective. From the religious practices of Wicca to the philosophies and doctrines of Celtic-Druids, it guides readers through each path with interesting facts and stories. Furthermore, readers gain a greater insight into Asatru, Slavic, and Germanic pagan cultures with details about their respective rituals, holidays, superstitions, and spirituality. While this book is perfect for anyone wanting to learn about the pagan culture or comparing multiple cultures side-by-side, it's invaluable to experienced neopagans seeking more information about their and others' beliefs.

If you are only just starting your spiritual quest or looking for an introduction to the fascinating world of Paganism, then Paganism for Beginners is perfect. It contains everything from basic information about this ancient practice to detailed accounts of powerful rituals for deepening spiritual connection. It is presented in easy-to-follow language, so even beginners can get started quickly without fuss or complication. So, why wait? Embark on your journey now.

Chapter 1: What Is Paganism?

Intuitively, Paganism is often misconstrued as a foreign belief system for many people. This chapter explores in greater detail what Paganism entails, who pagans were, and how neopagans have interpreted these beliefs today. While old pagan concepts are regularly linked to nature and powerful deities, they also incorporated special festivals into their traditions and rituals, signifying the changing of seasons throughout the year. From morality and ethical behavior to worshipful spirituality, pagan principles taught valuable life lessons while encouraging people to connect to a deeper life purpose.

Pagans had rituals for the change of seasons.[1]

Paganism

Paganism is an umbrella term to describe a wide range of spiritual and religious beliefs and practices based on pre-Christian traditions. It is typically polytheistic, meaning it involves worshiping multiple gods or goddesses. Paganism encompasses various modern and ancient belief systems, including those based on mythology, folklore, mysticism, and shamanism. These beliefs are animistic, meaning they view nature as alive and having its own spirit.

Paganism is based on a reverence for nature and a respect for the interconnectedness between all living things. It emphasizes personal responsibility, a balance between the physical and spiritual realms, respect for the wisdom of elders, and an openness to learning new things. Pagans believe divinity exists in all aspects of life, not only in deities but also in people, animals, objects, places, and plants.

Paganism has a rich history in many cultures worldwide. It can be seen in ancient Greek religion, Norse mythology, Celtic Paganism, Eastern European Slavic Paganism, Baltic Paganism, and Native American spirituality. It has been increasingly gaining traction in modern society as more people seek to reconnect with their ancestral roots through alternative spiritual practices.

Core Pagan beliefs include:

- Respect for nature and the environment
- Reverence for ancestors
- The interconnectedness of all life
- Balance between body, mind, and spirit
- Rituals to stay connected to the divine inner self
- Belief in magic
- Invocation of deities
- Use of symbolism as a means of communication with the divine
- Honoring male and female aspects of divinity (duotheism)
- A sense-related system rather than doctrine or dogma
- Living with intentionality rather than according to predetermined rules.

Pagans often practice their faith through ceremonies, such as handfasting (marriage ceremonies), sabbats (seasonal festivals), or esbats (Moon rituals). Common tools used during these ceremonies include candles, herbs, stones, and other nature-based items. There is no one "right way" to practice Paganism as each individual has their own interpretation of what it means.

Pagan Beliefs

The pagans of old were polytheistic, believing in multiple gods and goddesses who inhabited the natural world. They believed these gods and goddesses were responsible for the various aspects of life, such as fertility, death, war, love, and justice. Pagans saw themselves as connected with their gods and goddesses through a shared relationship between the divine and earthly realms.

Pagans deeply respected the natural world, believing all parts of nature, trees, rivers, mountains, and animals, were alive with spiritual energy. This spiritual energy was seen as divine forces at work in the environment and among all living things. Pagans often held rituals and offerings at sacred sites throughout the year to honor these spiritual energies.

Additionally, some pagans believed in reincarnation or rebirth after death based on a person's actions during their lifetime. This belief in karma meant a person would be rewarded or punished depending on how they lived their life. Pagans held to several tenets of morality, such as honoring ancestors and respecting nature's cycles. For them, morality was essential for maintaining balance in the world.

Pagan Thoughts on Cosmology

Pagan thoughts on creation or cosmology vary greatly between cultures. However, all pagan traditions share a common theme: understanding the interconnectedness of all life and the cyclical nature of existence.

In Greek mythology, creation began with Chaos. This primordial void was filled with potentiality, and out of it, Gaia (Earth), Tartarus (the underworld), Eros (love), and Night were born. Gaia gave birth to Uranus (sky), and they created the Titans and Cyclopes, who would later help create humans from clay. This idea of a divine couple creating all there hugely influenced ancient Greek culture, forming the basis for much mythology and art.

The Norse Pantheon consists of various gods, including Odin and Thor, responsible for shaping their world at the creation. According to Norse cosmology, this world was created when Ymir, a giant, emerged from the icy waters of Ginnungagap. The gods constructed Midgard (Earth) from his body parts while his blood became oceans, his brain created clouds, and his skull formed the sky. Additionally, these gods are responsible for controlling fate which can be seen in the stories of Ragnarok, where they battle against giants to restore order to the universe.

In Wicca, creation is part of an eternal cycle reflected in their version of the Wheel of the Year - eight festivals that mark major events throughout each season, such as Samhain or Mabon. These celebrations are a reminder that life isn't linear but moves in circles and comes full circle each year; people experience death so that new life can be born again. Wicca views life as sacred energy which exists within everything, including plants, animals, and rocks, so they believe it's important to respect all forms of life by living in balance with nature rather than trying to control it through technology or science.

Druidism is another form of Paganism that focuses on spirituality over theology but still has a unique view on creation or cosmology. One example is in their version of the Triad, the three elements which make up existence: fire, water, and air, respectively, representing passion and inspiration (fire), creativity (water), and power (air). These three elements work together in harmony to create balance in life, and why Druids focus heavily on ritualistic practices like meditation or chanting to keep these energies aligned within them to understand their place in the universe better.

Pagan beliefs on creation or cosmology vary greatly between cultures but generally involve a deep respect for cycles within nature or connections between divine beings who shape reality at its inception. Whether it's Chaos birthing Gaia or Ymir being used as foundations for Midgard by Odin and Thor, there is always an understanding that life is fragile. Yet it is constantly evolving due to powerful forces beyond human understanding that must be balanced if peace and harmony within self and the environment are to exist.

Pagan Deities

Pagan deities are gods and goddesses, often polytheistic, who are worshipped by followers of Paganism. These deities often represent natural forces, such as the Sun and Moon, fertility, love, death, and destruction. These deities were widely revered in ancient societies stretching from Europe to Asia Minor.

Examples of pagan deities include:
- The Greek Pantheon of gods and goddesses such as Zeus, Athena, Apollo, and Aphrodite
- Norse gods such as Odin, Thor, and Freya
- Celtic gods such as Lugh and Brigid
- Druidic figures like Cerridwen
- Hindu gods like Shiva and Vishnu
- Ancient Egyptian deities like Isis and Horus
- Mesopotamian gods like Marduk and Ishtar
- Persian gods like Ahura, Mazda, and Mithras
- Slavic deities like Perun and Veles.

The ancient Greeks believed their Pantheon of twelve Olympian gods was responsible for all aspects of life, from the mundane to the extraordinary. They controlled the weather, determined political events, and inspired great deeds of courage on the battlefields.

The major Greek gods included:
- Zeus (king of the gods)
- Poseidon (god of the sea)
- Hades (god of the underworld)
- Hera (queen of Olympus)
- Apollo (god of light)
- Hermes (messenger god)
- Aphrodite (goddess of love)
- Hestia (goddess of hearth)
- Athena (goddess of wisdom)
- Ares (god of war)
- Demeter (goddess of the harvest)
- Artemis (goddess of hunting).

In Norse mythology, Odin is considered All-Father or "the Father God," while Thor is regarded as "the Thunderer" or god associated with thunderstorms. Other important Norse gods are Freyja, a fertility goddess associated with magic and nature worship, and Balder, known as "the shining god" due to his beauty and goodness. Freyja is associated with fertility rites and rituals involving seiðr, an old shamanistic magic practiced in Northern Europe long before Christianity took root there.

The Celts worshiped numerous gods, including Dian Cecht, known for healing and arts, and Lugh, a powerful Sun god associated with protection and justice. Ancestor spirits were held in high regard by Celtic pagans. Druids believed them to be messengers between this world and the otherworld, where they interacted with spirit guides or ancestors when seeking guidance. Brigid was a powerful goddess associated with fire, poetry, writing, and metalworking. Cernunnos was one of the most popular deities among druids and was associated with animals and fertility rites.

In Hinduism, there are numerous gods, all representing different aspects. The three major ones are Brahma, creator god; Vishnu, protector god; and Shiva, destroyer god. The trinity concept comes from these three major gods representing different creation, preservation, and destruction aspects. Many other Hindu Gods include:

- Ganesha, an elephant-headed lord who removes obstacles
- Kali, or Parvati, has multiple forms depending on the region in which she is being worshipped
- Lakshmi, goddess of wealth and abundance
- Saraswati, goddess of music, knowledge, art, and education

The Ancient Egyptians had many gods representing natural forces. Pharaohs were seen as manifestations of several divine entities: Horus, the god sky; Ra, the solar deity; Isis, the goddess of motherhood and magic; and Osiris, the god of death and the afterlife.

Slavic mythology has several primary gods, almost all represented by trees: Perun, the thunderstorm god; Jarilo, the springtime warrior god; Kupala, the water handmaiden god; Morana, the goddess of winter; Veles, the ruler of the underworld; Stribog, the wind lord; Dazbog, the Sun chariot driver; and Radegast, the lord of hospitality.

Importance of Nature

Nature was extremely important to pagans because it symbolized life's sacred and divine power. For pagans, nature was considered a living entity infused with spiritual energy. Therefore, by engaging in rituals and ceremonies within nature, they could tap into this spiritual power and use it to bring balance and harmony to their lives. Pagans regarded nature as an embodiment of the gods, goddesses, and other deities they worshiped. They held festivals throughout the year to honor the deities and pay homage to them in accordance with the natural cycles of life.

In addition to its spiritual significance for pagans, nature was a source of practical necessities, such as shelter, food, medicine, and clothing. By relying on nature for survival, pagans developed a deep respect for it, further contributing to its importance in their lives. Furthermore, pagan societies were largely agrarian-based, meaning their livelihoods were inextricably linked to nature's bounty. This connection strengthened their reverence for nature. Life cycles within nature (birth and death, growth and decay) were seen as symbols of transformation and renewal, serving as reminders that life is sacred and should be respected.

For example, in ancient Greece, the god Pan represented all aspects of nature through his connection to the woods and wilds. He was known as the god of fertility, shepherding, and even music, symbolizing how nature could provide sustenance and joy in equal measures. Nature was a source of healing and transformation for physical ailments or spiritual needs. The Oracle at Delphi drew upon natural elements, such as trees, water springs, and smoke from sacrificed animals, to gain insight into questions from the people who visited her from across Greece.

In Norse culture, nature was essential for understanding the world around them. The gods were often associated with certain elements of nature: Odin with wind (and battle), Thor with thunder (and protection), and Freya with fertility (and love). It linked deities to specific forces to explain why certain events happened in their lives. It helped them understand their environment, including unpredictable weather patterns, crop failures, and animal migrations.

The Wicca revere nature just as much. They believe it is connected to divine energy because it can give life and take it away if not respected properly. They hold rituals within natural settings like forests or meadows to honor the Earth's spirit while seeking guidance or protection. Wiccans use plants for spells and potions while celebrating important seasonal transitions throughout the year, connecting themselves spiritually with cycles like those in animals or plants.

Druids venerated trees and forests, believing they had healing powers and could communicate messages between themselves and their gods.

Overall, for these pagan cultures, nature provided an avenue toward understanding life's mysteries. By observing cycles within its vastness, they could draw connections between their faiths and everyday experiences more easily than modern-day religions typically allow. Nature was essential for survival during difficult times yet could provide hope for a better tomorrow, making it highly valued by these ancient societies.

Pagan Seasons and Festival

Pagans celebrated the seasons' cycles and the changing of light and dark throughout the year. The festivals, or holy days, usually began at sundown on the evening before and lasted for several days.

The Wheel of the Year was a cycle of eight festivals known as sabbats. Each marked an important time in nature's cycle and a celebration held during that time.

The sabbats were:

- Imbolc (Feb 1st)
- Ostara (spring equinox, around Mar 21st)
- Beltane (May 1st)
- Litha (summer solstice, around June 21st)
- Lammas (Aug 1st)
- Mabon (autumn equinox, around Sep 22nd)
- Samhain (Nov 1st)
- Yule (winter solstice, around Dec 21st)

During each season, pagans would come together to pay homage to their gods, thank Mother Nature for her bounty, and honor their ancestors gone before them.

At Imbolc, pagans celebrated the returning light after winter's long darkness. It is ushered in with fire ceremonies, honoring Brigid and lighting candles to signify her strength. They would chant blessings over seeds ready to be planted in the springtime soil, a symbolic way of honoring natural cycles.

Ostara marks the point where night and day are equal, known as balance or harmony between light and dark energies. It is traditionally celebrated with rituals involving eggs, a symbol of new life emerging from darkness. Many pagans gather in a circle and share stories about new beginnings while exchanging colored eggs filled with symbols of good fortune for each other.

At Mabon, which marks the autumn equinox when day turns into night again, pagans reflect on how far they have come since spring's first light. Harvest time has arrived, so ample opportunities exist for feasting on freshly gathered fruits and vegetables. It is common to bake bread using grains harvested during this period or make offerings out of apples, food associated with the fertility goddess Demeter who presides over Mabon celebrations.

Samhain marks the end of summer's growth and abundance and the start of winter's long chill. Pagans honor their ancestors by hosting rituals to help their spirits find peace on this plane rather than linger among mortals longer than necessary. People prepare foods like apple pies or roasted root vegetables as offerings to deceased loved ones. These offerings were thought to nourish souls when they needed it most during their journey beyond life's physical realm into the spirit world.

Neopaganism and Their Modern-Day Beliefs

Neopaganism is a modern spiritual movement that seeks to reconnect with pre-Christian, indigenous religions' ancient beliefs and practices. Neopagans attempt to revive and recreate the rituals, sacred sites, gods, and goddesses of the old world. They draw on many sources, including archaeological evidence, folk traditions, and historical texts. While many neopagan groups share some common core beliefs, each has unique customs and practices.

The term "neopagan" was first used in the 1950s by George Russell in his book "The Worship of Nature," which sought to bring together various strands of Paganism. Since then, neopaganism has taken on a life of its own as various groups have sought to revive the religion within their cultural context. Neopagans embrace several belief systems, including Wicca, Druidry, Shamanism, Celtic Reconstructionism, and Heathenism. They often practice seasonal or lunar celebrations known as sabbats or esbats to connect them with their ancestors and nature cycles. Many neopagans practice magic or spellwork for healing or protection, including herbal remedies or spells using the four elements (earth, air, fire, and water).

Neopagans adhere to an ethical code based on an awareness of the interconnectedness between people and all other creatures in nature (referred to as "the web of life"). Therefore, many neopagans seek to live in harmony with nature by avoiding activities like burning fossil fuels or over-hunting animals and engaging in conservation efforts like planting trees or cleaning beaches. Neopagans are highly concerned with environmental issues, such as global warming, pollution, and species extinction due to human activity.

Many neopagan groups emphasize community building. They believe it is important to come together regularly with friends and family to celebrate their faith and enjoy each other's company. These gatherings often involve feasting (including vegetarian dishes), storytelling, singing, dancing, drumming, painting, music, rituals, bonfires, and other activities celebrating life rather than a particular deity or event.

Whether modern-day neopagans hold similar beliefs and conduct similar customs or practices to their predecessors depends largely on what they consider "predecessors." For example, some contemporary Wiccans draw heavily from ancient Celtic tradition, while others draw from Norse Heathenism. Both differ from traditional Hinduism despite having some shared concepts, such as worshiping multiple deities or revering nature's cycles. Similarly, different branches of Druids have different beliefs about the afterlife; for instance, Hindus might not consider an afterlife (or have differing views, depending on sects).

Many contemporary neopagan practices align closely with those from ancient times.

- Honoring various gods and goddesses
- Sacred sites
- Ancestor veneration
- Seasonal festivals
- Oral traditions
- Natural objects used ritualistically
- Meditation
- Divination

- Herbal remedies
- Animal sacrifice
- Offerings
- Wild dancing
- Trances
- Drumming
- Chanting
- Poetry
- Mask making

Additionally, many neopagans focus heavily on specific deities, like Odin, Freya, Brigid, Athena, and Apollo. These gods often have specific associated characteristics celebrated through religious observances, characteristic behaviors, customary chants, mythologies, artwork, tales and stories, and symbols. Of course, even among those who practice similar beliefs, there are variations depending on individual preference, culture, society, and region. Therefore, when discussing similarities between modern-day neopagans, there will always be differences between individuals or groups. However, most neopagans honor certain core principles, such as respect for nature, honoring female and male gods, maintaining a connection with ancestors, and celebrating life and death cycles.

Chapter 2: Celtic Paganism and Druidry

The terms Celtic Paganism and Druidry are often used interchangeably. Both beliefs originated from similar European countries, like Ireland and Scotland, and shared many similarities. However, they aren't the same, and their differences give each belief its own identity and characteristics.

This chapter explains Druidry and Celtic Paganism, highlights their differences, and discusses Celtic myths, deities, rituals, and festivals.

Celtic Paganism vs. Druidry

The Celts were a group of tribes from central Europe who shared the same language, culture, traditions, and religious beliefs. Interestingly, modern scholars referred to them as "Celts," but no one knows what they were originally called. It is believed each tribe had its own name rather than having an umbrella term like the Greek or Roman empires.

They practiced Celtic Paganism, an ancient polytheistic religion that worshiped more than one deity and spiritual practices and beliefs. They believed their gods existed in everything around them, so they highly revered nature.

Druidry, called Druidism, was a shamanic religion that originated in Britain, particularly Wales. It involved communicating and working with the spirits and belief in the power of holistic medicine in causing and treating diseases. The religion was part of the Celtic culture hence its association with Celtic Paganism. It was a religious belief and a magical practice.

The Druids considered oak trees sacred.²

The druids were Celtic priests and leaders of the Celtic religion and Druidry. The word "*druid*" is derived from the Celtic word "*doire*," meaning oak tree or wisdom. The druids considered the oak tree the most sacred of all trees.

They were extremely wise and knowledgeable and acted as judges, philosophers, scholars, and doctors, connecting people to their deities. They played a huge role in Celtic society; kings and peasants often sought their wisdom. Unfortunately, the druids passed down their teachings orally and prohibited their followers and students from using the written word. As a result, most information scholars have about Celtic Paganism and druids is second-hand knowledge.

Julius Caesar invaded Britain in 55 BC. He witnessed the druids and their influence firsthand. In his book, "The Gallic Wars," he mentioned that they were key figures in the Celtic faith, performed religious duties, interpreted all aspects of the religion, and were highly respected among the people who often turned to them to settle disputes. They even used their influence to prevent wars. He added that when a person committed a crime, the druids had the power to pass judgment.

Caesar also mentioned in his book how the druids urged their members to memorize all their teachings and religious beliefs instead of writing them down because they didn't want their knowledge to spread among the commoners.

The druids were so powerful and untouchable that the Celtic laws and rules didn't apply to them. For instance, they didn't serve in the army or pay taxes. They were different from the Celtic pagans, the same way a regular person differs from a priest. They influenced the people with their knowledge and power, and the Celtic pagans sought their help with all matters.

Both religions believed in the afterlife, worshiping multiple deities, and highly revered nature, so people often confuse the two. Celtic Paganism is a broad term describing all pagans in the Celtic society, including the druids. However, *Druidry* refers to a group of people within the Celts. In other words, all druids were Celtic pagans but not all Celtic pagans were druids. Druidry focused more on nature and magic than mythology and cosmology, which were significant in Celtic Paganism.

Nowadays, Druidry is a spiritual path and a way of life, but some people still treat it as a religion. It became a diverse belief welcoming people from all religions, including Celtic pagans. However, not all are polytheists. They can also be monotheists (worshiping one god), duotheistic (worshiping two gods), pantheists (believing god is the universe), or animists (believing everything has a spirit, including inanimate objects). However, one thing they all have in common is that nature is sacred, a belief they share with their ancient ancestors.

Neo-Celtic pagans or Celtic Reconstructionism is based on ancient Celtic beliefs and incorporating its practices into modern society. Similar to their ancestors, they are polytheistic and revere nature. It is separate from neo-Druidry as each religion has its own identity.

The Celtic Belief System and Spirituality

The Celtic pagans highly revered nature, especially trees they considered sacred, and worshiped their deities in natural settings like cliffs, bushes, rivers, and lakes. They held the Moon, stars, and Sun in high regard and believed them supernatural. They considered animals like horses, bulls, stags, and boars sacred and often engraved them on armor and weapons for protection.

The Celtic pagans worshiped over 400 gods and goddesses and appeased their deities by offering them their favorite food, drinks, weapons, and valuable objects. Unlike ancient Roman and Greek deities, they didn't have human characteristics. In other words, they didn't have weaknesses, nor were they influenced by worldly desires. The Celts believed the deities controlled the universe and mankind and hugely influenced people's daily lives.

Since the Celts revered nature, they associated their gods and goddesses with natural settings and phenomena like lightning and the Sun. Many of their deities were depicted as a trio representing three divinity aspects. For instance, the goddess Matronae was a triple goddess associated with fertility, power, and strength.

Although they had a deity for everything like the Moon, Sun, hospitality, and chance, the main focus was on the gods and goddesses associated with the main concerns of people, like protection, healing, warfare, hunting, and tribal identity.

They believed in supernatural beings like elves and fairies who existed in nature and were very powerful creatures. They could help and bless mankind, but if mistreated, they would reveal their ugly side and cause harm and disease.

The Celts believed in the afterlife, which is clear from their burial rituals. They buried the royals and the rich with all their belongings, such as food, utensils, pottery, jewelry, clothes, board games, armor, weapons, and everything else needed for their journey to the underworld. Their leaders and prominent individuals in the state were buried in wood-lined chambers and dressed in their best attire.

Although not much is known about their afterlife, scholars believe the Celts regarded the otherworld as the same as this life but without its negative aspects like grief, pain, loss, and diseases. As a result, they didn't fear death and welcomed its arrival. Cremation was common in ancient Paganism, which they borrowed from Mediterranean cultures.

Myths and Cosmology

Understanding the cosmology of the Celtic religion, its deities, and sacred symbols can only be done through myths and legends. Like many ancient cultures, the Celts had a rich and fascinating mythology, and people still tell their stories in Ireland, Wales, and various parts of Europe.

King Arthur's Journey to Annwn (The Spoils of Annwn)

This legend is based on the poem "Preiddeu Annwn." Preiddeu means spoils, and Annwn means the underworld. King Arthur took his men and three ships and traveled to the underworld to take a cauldron that belonged to the lord of Annwn. The cauldron had magical powers. It would only boil the food of the brave, not the coward.

Arthur arrived at Caer Sidi, the fort of the otherworld or the fairy fortress. He found the cauldron in a cave over a fire with nine maidens breathing over it to keep it burning.

The poem is very mysterious and dark. One line echoed in multiple stanzas, "Except seven, none returned," indicated that only Arthur and six of his men survived this disastrous journey. However, he returned victoriously with the cauldron.

Interestingly, the poem doesn't only reflect Arthur's bravery and his ability to survive the journey to the underworld, but it also highlights the cauldron's significance in Celtic mythology. One of the most famous cauldrons belonged to Cerridwen, a mythical Celtic witch and the goddess of inspiration. She used it to make magical potions that bestowed wisdom and knowledge on whoever drank them. The cauldron could resurrect the dead.

Cerridwen's cauldron appeared in another legend with Bran the Blessed, the giant King of Wales. He gave it as a wedding gift to his sister Branwen and her husband Math, the King of Ireland. However, when war broke out between Wales and Ireland, Bran decided to take back the cauldron. The story shared many similarities with the legend of King Arthur. Bran also took the journey with some of his bravest knights, but only seven survived. He died in battle and went to the underworld like King Arthur in the Quest of the Holy Grail, who went to Avalon after his death. Some scholars believe Cerridwen's cauldron is the Holy Grail that King Arthur searched for all his life.

The Legend of the Tuatha Dé Danann

The Tuatha Dé Danann were the tribes of gods in Celtic cosmology. Before they arrived in Ireland, a group of giants called the Firbolgs ruled the land. The Firbolgs were surprised by the arrival of the Tuatha Dé Danann and weren't prepared for battle, making it easy for the gods to vanquish them and rule Ireland. Their King Nuada, the god of hunting, was badly hurt during the battle and lost his arm. It made him unfit to rule because, according to the Tuatha Dé Danann laws, the king should be in perfect health and shape.

Although the other gods loved and respected him, Nuada had no choice but to step down from the throne. He appointed Breas to take his place but only for seven years until Nuada found a way to restore his arm. Breas's mother was from the Tuatha Dé Danann, but his father belonged to the Fomorians, a group of monstrous giants. Breas was a vicious and unfair king who favored the Fomorians over the Tuatha Dé Danann during his rule.

Creidhne, the god of metalworkers, succeeded in creating a silver hand for Nuada. The king returned to his kingdom and took back his throne. Although Breas knew his position was temporary, he was angry when he had to give up the throne. However, the people rejoiced since they loathed him and loved Nuada. Breas went to Balor, the leader of the Fomorians, to sow the seeds of war between the two tribes. Balor agreed to fight the gods. Some of the Firbolgs joined them since they wanted to get back at the Tuatha Dé Danann for taking their kingdom. Although he had one eye, Balor was a very strong and cruel giant. He fought hard in the battle, killing many of the Tuatha Dé Danann, including their King Nuada.

Lugh, the god of justice, nobility, and the Sun, was a powerful and honorable deity and the grandson of Balor. Although he was half Fomorian from his mother's side, he was nothing like Breas. Nuada trusted him and chose him to lead the army. Lugh proved to be a great leader. He used his magic to strengthen the army and provided them with weapons.

When Lugh found out on the battlefield that his grandfather killed Nuada, he was adamant about avenging his king. He killed Balor, leading to the Tuatha Dé Danann's victory.

Lugh became a hero and was chosen to rule the Tuatha Dé Danann. He was a just, brave, and wise king. He used his kinship with the Fomorians to establish peace between the two races.

The Main Gods and Goddesses in Celtic Paganism

Lugh

Lugh was the god of judgment, oaths, and nobility and one of Celtic Paganism's most popular and strongest deities. He had many titles, but the most famous was Lámfada, meaning "of the long arm." It referred to the magical and powerful spear he often used on the battlefield. He was a king, judge, and poet known for his many skills. The god was responsible for distributing talents among mankind. Caesar mentioned him in his books as one of the most prominent gods in Celtic Paganism and highly revered among the people.

Interestingly, Lugh was a trickster deity who would steal, cheat, and lie to defeat his opponents.

When Lugh wanted to join the court of Nuada, he traveled a long road to reach Tara, the hall of the kings. When he asked to enter, the guard told him he must have a unique skill to be allowed in the court. Lugh showed him his many skills as a poet, blacksmith, wheelwright, and many others. However, the guard told him they already had someone with that particular talent each time. Lugh used his wit and told the guard they didn't have a champion with all these skills. The guard realized Lugh was right and let him in the court. It was in the court where he proved himself and impressed Nuada to the extent that he became the leader of his army.

The Morrigan

The Morrigan (or *Morrighan*) was the goddess of fate, battles, wars, and death. She supported Celtic heroes and gods, helped the Tuatha Dé Danann in battle, and prophesied their victory against the Fomorians. She could transform into a beautiful woman to lure men or into a raven and fly over the battlefields. It is believed if she appeared to a warrior in the water while he washed his armor, he would die that day in battle. She had the power to decide who lived and died during a war.

According to some legends, she was a triple goddess. Nemain, Macha, and Badb were three goddesses called the Morrigan. However, in other legends, they were her sisters.

One of the most famous myths associated with the Morrigan is her story with Cu Chulainn, a mighty warrior, and Lugh's son. Cu Chulainn was at war with Queen Maeve, protecting the Irish city of Ulster from the queen's army. The Morrigan, who was always present on battlefields, fell in love with the young warrior when she first saw him. She transformed into a beautiful woman to seduce him right before the battle, but he rejected her advances.

The Morrigan was furious and vowed vengeance against the man who broke her heart. She transformed into an eel, swam to Cu Chulainn, and attacked him. However, the strong warrior punched the eel, not knowing it was the goddess, and hurt it badly. She recovered fast, transformed into a wolf, and drove a herd of cattle to Cu Chulainn. He hit the fox in the eye with a slingshot, blinding the Morrigan.

The determined goddess transformed again into a cow and drove a herd of cows to stampede the young warrior. He survived the attack and broke the Morrigan's leg. Cu Chulainn finally went to battle and won.

On his way home, he saw an elderly woman milking a cow. She had one broken leg and was blinded in one eye. He conversed with her, and she offered him a glass of milk. After drinking the milk, he blessed the woman, which cured her of all the injuries. The woman was the Morrigan, who tricked Cu Chulainn into healing her.

On his way to another battle, he saw a woman washing bloody armor, which was a bad omen. However, he didn't let the image deter him and continued his journey to the battle.

Unfortunately, the brave hero was mortally wounded, but he managed to tie himself upright to a large stone to scare his enemies. While taking his last breath, a crow landed on his shoulder. Was it the Morrigan? No one knows.

The Dagda

The Dagda was the Tuatha dé Danann chief and the father deity of Ireland. He was the god of Druidry, magic, fertility, agriculture, seasons, knowledge, life, and death. Druids highly revered him since he bestowed on them wisdom and knowledge of magic. He was the most powerful and skilled of all the Celtic deities, and his name meant the good god.

He was often depicted carrying a club in one hand that could end and resurrect someone's life and a magic cauldron over his shoulder containing an endless supply of food. He also carried a harp which he used to change the seasons.

The Dagda was the husband of the Morrigan and the brother of Nuada. He was mortally wounded during the battle against the Fomorians at the hands of Balor's wife, Cethlenn.

Brigid

Brigid (also spelled *Brighid)* was the Dagda's daughter and the goddess of life, fertility, motherhood, passion, fire, water, serenity, and spring. She was associated with poetry and healing. Like the Morrigan, she was a triple goddess, with two other goddesses also called Brigid. Her name meant "the exalted one." She is often compared with the Catholic saint Brigid since they both have more in common than just their names. Ancient and modern Celt pagans celebrate the goddess during the Imbolc festival in February. She hugely influenced people by inspiring poets and writers and protecting newborns and mothers.

During the battle between the Tuatha dé Danann and the Fomorians, Brigid lost her father and her son Ruadán. When she heard the news, she ran to the battlefield and saw her son's lifeless body. Her heart was broken, and she wailed in a loud lament that became known as keening. It was the first time someone expressed their grief in that manner, and everyone in Ireland felt her pain. It is how keening became a tradition among Irish women mourning their dead.

Cernunnos

Cernunnos was referred to as the horned god, the deity of wild places and beasts, and the protector of the forests. He ruled over nature and animals and was associated with vegetation and fertility. He was a mysterious god, and only a few things were known about him.

As a result of his association with animals and forests, Cernunnos led an uncivilized life. The animals were his servants, and he was often depicted as surrounded by snakes, wolves, and elks. He could tame animals and bring predators and prey together.

The Celtic Festivals

The Celtic calendar is called the Wheel of the Year. All Celtic festivals focused on seasonal changes since they impacted agriculture and harvest.

Samhain (October 31)

Samhain celebrated the end of summer and the harvest season. The veil between the realm of the living and the dead is weak during this time, allowing ancestors' spirits to travel to this world. People would often place an extra plate on the dinner table to remember and honor their departed loved ones. Halloween and its traditions were all borrowed from Samhain.

Yule (Winter Solstice December 20-23)

Yule takes place on the shortest day of the year and is a time of rebirth and renewal. People light candles and bonfires to celebrate the Sun's return during this festival. It is similar to Christmas and includes decorations like trees and mistletoe.

Imbolc (February 2)

This festival takes place between winter and spring and celebrates the goddess Brigid. It also celebrates the end of the winter and the arrival of spring. People would light candles and place them in every room to represent the Sun's return.

Ostara (Spring Equinox March 20-23)

Ostara represents new beginnings and celebrates the arrival of spring and the end of darkness. It is similar to Easter and shares the same traditions, like decorating eggs.

Bealtaine (May 1)

Bealtaine celebrates spring, warm weather, and all nature's gifts. During this festival, people light bonfires for protection against evil forces and celebrate by dancing. Many couples get married on this day because it is associated with passion and lust.

Summer Solstice (June 20-23)

This festival takes place on the longest day of the year during the warm weather when nature is strongest. People celebrate outdoors, throw feasts, eat delicious food, and light bonfires. The fairies are usually active during this time, so people leave them offerings.

Lughnasadh (August 1)

This festival is associated with the god Lugh who threw a feast and held competitions to honor his foster mother, Tailtiu, the goddess of labor and childbirth. She was responsible for clearing the fields so mankind could harvest their plants. However, it was a hard process, and she died. Therefore, Lugh honored her with this festival. People celebrated it by lighting bonfires.

Mabon (Autumn Equinox September 20-23)

Mabon takes place when the day is equal to the night. During these days, the Sun weakens in preparation for winter. People express their gratitude for the harvest and all nature's blessings.

A Simple Ritual to Do at Home

Create a spring altar at home during Bealtaine to celebrate the festival. You can use the altar for worship and prayers all year long.

Instructions:

1. Choose a room or a small space in your home away from distractions.
2. Clean it from dust and cleanse the area with burning sage (burn a bundle of sage and let the smoke purify the area).
3. Place a white cloth over the altar.

4. Add candles, fresh flowers, statues, symbols, or pictures of your favorite Celtic deity and nature symbols. Keep it simple.
5. Write your intentions for the rest of the year on a piece of paper and leave it on the altar.
6. Light a candle every day to energize the altar and reaffirm your intentions.
7. Don't ignore your altar and keep it maintained.

Disclaimer: Burning sage and candles are fire hazards, so caution is advised.

Celtic Paganism is a rich and fascinating religion. Each god has a different personality, power, and domain, adding to the religion's magic and allurement. Many things can be learned from Druidry and Celtic Paganism, like respecting nature and animals and believing that mankind isn't superior but one with all the gods' creations.

Chapter 3: Asatru: Norse Paganism

Asatru Paganism is a fascinating and mysterious practice that has existed since before the Viking era. It is the modern interpretation of ancient Norse belief systems, blending spiritual practices with mythology, rituals, and ethical beliefs. This chapter delves into the specifics of Asatru Paganism, exploring its origins and cosmology, discussing its spirituality and beliefs, naming the gods and goddesses they pray to, and introducing readers to their rituals. Whether or not you subscribe to the spiritual teachings of Asatru Paganism, it is an intriguing way to trace the roots back through history, uncovering past traditions.

What Is Asatru?

Asatru is a modern revival of the ancient pre-Christian belief system of the Icelandic people, commonly known as Norse Paganism. This spiritual tradition dates back to the first century CE and was practiced by many Germanic tribes living in Northern Europe. The religion was almost completely forgotten until its revival in the late 19th century.

The origins of Asatru can be traced to Old Norse literature, particularly the Eddas, which are collections of ancient stories and poetry chronicling religious beliefs and historical events from Scandinavian cultures. These texts describe the gods and goddesses worshiped by these tribes and their cosmology and rituals. In particular, they talk about Odin and his brothers, Vili and Ve, creating the world from nothingness on Yggdrasil (the World Tree). They provide insight into how various magical runes were used for divination, healing practices, and other traditional customs, such as feasting on holidays like Yule (the winter solstice) or celebrating Freyr's Day around the summer solstice period.

The origins of Asatru can be traced to the Eddas.[8]

In addition to this literary evidence, archaeological excavations discovered artifacts suggesting that these belief systems were incredibly widespread during this period, from Sweden down to what are now Germany, Austria, Hungary, and parts of Romania. For example, bronze figurines depicting Odin were found throughout Scandinavia dating back to 600 CE, while grave goods, like swords, were discovered in graves, depicting Viking-era burial practices.

The revival of Asatru began in Iceland in 1972 with Sveinbjörn Beinteinsson leading an initiative known as "The Ásatrúarfélagið" (or "Ásatrú Fellowship"). This organization sought to restore traditional beliefs and practices under a new name, Ásatrú, meaning "faith in the gods." Since then, various organizations have been established around Europe, including Norway's Foreningen for Nordisk Religions (FNR), Denmark's Forn Siðr/Nordisk Hedendom, Britain's Odinic Rite/The Odinic Rite Association (ORA), and Germany's Ring der Götter und Geister (RiGG). Despite its relatively recent revival, compared to other belief systems like Christianity or Islam, Asatru has quickly become one of the largest religions, with millions of adherents worldwide practicing their faith according to its core tenets.

Cosmology

The cosmology of Asatru is a subject that its adherents have fiercely debated. The religion heavily focuses on the Norse Pantheon and its various myths and stories. At its heart, Asatru centers on the concept of honor, not only for yourself but also for all living things. This honor is expressed primarily through reverence for the gods and goddesses in the Norse Pantheon and adherence to a heroic code of conduct known as "the Nine Noble Virtues."

At its core, Asatru recognizes nine realms:

- The three worlds beneath Earth, Niflheim, Muspellsheim, and Svartalfheim
- Midgard (the world)
- Jotunheim (a realm occupied by giants)
- Asgard (home of the gods)
- Vanaheim (the realm of the Vanir gods)
- Alfheim (the realm of the light elves)
- Helheim (the underworld)

Within these realms live numerous beings, such as dwarves, elves, giants, gods, and goddesses. Each realm is inhabited by its spiritual entities, including deities and other supernatural figures with specific areas of influence relevant to human life.

The relationship between humans and these divine entities determines their fates in this life and their afterlife. In Asatru belief systems, humans are part of an interconnected web of existence where every action affects them somehow. Therefore, it is important to maintain a balance within this web to achieve spiritual and physical harmony.

Asatru has two components: faith in Odin and other Norse deities and a warrior ethic requiring followers to meet challenges head-on with courage and strength. This warrior ethos greatly emphasizes courage, sacrifice, personal honor, strength in battle, and loyalty to friends or clan members.

Beliefs and Spirituality

Ásatrú, and the closely related Norse Paganism, is a polytheistic faith venerating many gods and goddesses. It is rooted in pre-Christian practices in Viking Age Scandinavia but has been influenced by modern interpretations of Norse mythos from sources like the Poetic Edda and Prose Edda. Asatru. Norse Paganism is based on the belief that deities are living beings with whom followers can interact directly, often through rituals or offerings. The gods are seen as protectors or guardians of humanity, and their worship helps ensure success and prosperity. In addition to the Pantheon of gods, adherents venerate land spirits (*landvaettir*), ancestors (*disir*), and various other spirits.

Asatru - Norse Paganism is a faith that celebrates nature's power in all forms and seeks to maintain a balance between humanity and the gods. The religion aims to live harmoniously with the gods and nature. Practitioners believe everything around them is alive and sacred, from rocks to trees, rivers, oceans, fire, animals, and birds. Everything has an elemental spirit that can be honored if respected.

At its heart, Asatru is an animistic religion. Adherents see everything around them, from animals and plants to mountains and rivers, as having their own spirits, energies, or powers. Animism is reflected in many customs, such as offering libations to land spirits when entering new territories or asking permission from tree spirits before cutting down trees.

Asatru practitioners believe fate is predetermined by a person's actions in past lives (*wyrd*) or how others affect you (*orþrótt*). Therefore, every action has good and bad consequences, so people should strive for righteousness to ensure good fortune for now and in future lifetimes. This belief ties into one of the core values held by Asatru, honor your word (*hlautbúa*). Being honorable means being truthful with yourself and others which helps build trust between people while maintaining respect for yourself by keeping your promises.

The gods and goddesses of Asatru are integral components of this belief system. They represent various facets of nature and humanity, such as fertility, war, justice, family life, death, love, and wisdom. These deities are viewed as powerful supernatural beings and role models whose stories provide insight into how humans should conduct themselves. Worshiping these gods brings blessings if done properly. However, neglecting them can bring misfortune or tragedy to yourself and those around you.

The gods are considered distinct entities with their wills and personalities. They are viewed as spiritual forces rather than abstract concepts or metaphors. In addition, rituals are associated with honoring the gods, such as blot sacrifices where animals were partially or wholly sacrificed as food offerings during celebrations like Yule or Winternights (*Hallowtide*). These ceremonies were thought necessary for maintaining relationships between humans and their deities, allowing them access to Valhalla after death. Upon their deaths in battle or from natural causes, they would be welcomed into Odin's hall. Other rituals pertain specifically to holidays like Ostara, where eggs were exchanged between family members signifying renewal, and Thor was honored by lit bonfires on Midsummer night. These rituals were meant to honor the gods and as a reminder that living harmoniously among each other is possible if faithfully adhering to values with those sharing the same beliefs.

By honoring the gods through ritual, adherents seek to live according to the moral code of Asatru - Norse Paganism: The Nine Noble Virtues. The Nine Noble Virtues of Norse Paganism, known as Asatru, are moral codes guiding and shaping the conduct of practitioners. These virtues come from an ancient pagan religion and are still practiced today.

1. **Courage:** To be courageous in all situations, take risks, accept challenges with strength, and be resilient in times of difficulty.
2. **Truth:** To live honestly and openly, never lie or deceive others, and strive for truth.
3. **Honor:** To maintain a noble character at all times, uphold the highest standards of behavior with integrity, and strive for excellence in everything.
4. **Fidelity:** To remain true to your word, relationships, and commitments - and stand by loyal friends and family.
5. **Discipline:** To practice self-control, stay focused on achieving goals, and practice moderation.

6. **Hospitality**: To provide generous hospitality when hosting guests and treat them as honored family members.
7. **Industriousness:** To work hard to gain knowledge, develop skills, earn money, build material wealth, and always improve self.
8. **Self-Reliance**: To rely on self rather than depending on others, take responsibility for your actions, and not rely on luck or fate.
9. **Perseverance:** To remain strong despite adversity and never give up, even when faced with great hardship or opposition.

Another important aspect of Asatru spirituality is saga telling, stories about mythological characters from Norse lore, usually around a campfire after dinner at private gatherings or ritual events. Through listening to these tales, participants learn more about their culture's history while discovering spiritual lessons within their narratives about heroism, courage, loyalty, self-sacrifice, honor, justice, truthfulness, compassion, humility, and wisdom. Furthermore, these tales offer insight into how adherents should live according to a worldview based on Nordic traditions. It helps adherents become better versed in integral aspects of Heathenry's values, ethics, morals, and laws.

Significantly, Asatru - Norse Paganism is an ever-evolving faith tradition. Today's beliefs and practices span from humanism to Reconstructionism, from viewing the gods as metaphorical constructs to approaching them as distinct beings. The diversity of belief within the community allows followers to explore their spiritual paths while honoring their cultural heritage and connecting with other pagans globally. Regardless of how you view or practice Asatru - Norse Paganism, its fundamental core is an appreciation for life and nature and a commitment to working toward a balance in the physical and spiritual worlds. With this understanding, adherents can strive toward living a meaningful life filled with joy, wisdom, and fulfillment.

Gods and Goddesses

Asatru, or Norse Paganism, is based on the belief in multiple gods and goddesses who inhabit different realms and guide humanity. Many gods and goddesses are associated with Asatru, but some are more important than others. These major deities include Odin, Thor, Freya, Freyja, Frigg, Loki, Heimdall, and Idunn. These major gods and goddesses are closely linked to Asatru beliefs and are essential to Norse Paganism. They guide, protect and offer wisdom to their people while being respected as powerful deities. By understanding these deities more, practitioners can better appreciate aspects of the faith, such as its mythology and symbolism.

1. Odin

Odin is considered the chief god of Asatru. He is known as a powerful deity who rules over Asgard, the realm of the Aesir gods. He is a wise teacher who gives advice and wisdom to humankind through prophetic revelations. Odin is associated with war and magic. It is said that he sacrificed his eye to gain wisdom. Odin had magical powers allowing him to shape-shift into animals or people. He carried two magical artifacts, an eight-legged horse named Sleipnir, which could travel between worlds without getting tired, and an all-seeing eye called Odin's Eye, which allowed him to see into many places simultaneously.

2. Thor

Thor is Odin's son and the primary god of thunder in Asatru mythology. Thor is the god of thunder and lightning and rules over storms. He is one of the most famous figures in Norse mythology. Known for his strength and courage, he could wield a magical hammer called Mjölnir, which controlled lightning bolts. Thor protects Asgard from giants who attack it, using his magical hammer to strike them down. He is a guardian of humankind, protecting them from harm and helping them through difficult times.

3. Freya

Freya is a goddess of love, beauty, fertility, and war in the Asatru Pantheon. She has many associations with nature, such as fertility, love, and sexuality. Freya is a strong protector of her people, particularly those most vulnerable. She often takes the form of a beautiful falcon when in battle, leading warriors to victory.

4. Freyja

Freyja is Freya's twin sister and is associated with similar aspects like fertility and love. She wears a necklace of precious stones called Brisingamen, which grants her great powers. Freyja's power lies in her ability to see into the future and guide mankind. Freyja has the power to cause strife among enemies if someone wrongs her or her loved ones. She can take on different shapes at will and travels around Midgard (the realm of humans) on her chariot pulled by cats.

5. Frigg

Frigg is Odin's wife and goddess of marriage and motherhood in Asatru mythology. Like Freya and Freyja, she is associated with love and fertility. She is a wise and loving mother figure who looks after all Asgard's inhabitants.

6. Freyr

Freyr is one of the Vanir gods associated with peace, fertility, and prosperity in Norse mythology associated with peace. Freyr was known for his great wealth but was generous, giving away his possessions freely even when it led him into trouble or danger. He gave away his last valuable possession, his magical sword, to win over Gerd (a giantess), whom he wanted to marry. He was renowned for having an enormous appetite. It became a running joke among other gods and goddesses that he was never satisfied – no matter how much food they served him.

7. Tyr

Tyr was another god associated with war, specifically for courage and bravery on battlefields. Tyr offered warriors strength and courage when their natural reserves were depleted. Tyr was admired by many for his selfless actions like bravery. He sacrificed one hand, so the Fenrir wolf would not break free from its bonds, preventing *Ragnarok* (the twilight age and the end of the world) from happening prematurely.

8. Loki

Loki isn't technically considered a deity but an immortal trickster who caused much mischief throughout the Norse Pantheon. He is depicted as sometimes playing pranks and other times causing destruction and malice purposely. However, Loki's primary function is to nurture humankind, ultimately assisting birth and the new beginning after Ragnarök.

9. Heimdall

Heimdall is the Aesir race's herald protector. He is in charge of guarding the Bifrost Bridge connecting the Asgard realm to mortals' Midgard. His sharp, keen senses allow him to detect even the slightest disturbance miles away, making perfect sense of why he is appointed sentry of the gateway between realms.

10. Idunn

Idunn is the goddess of youth and immortality in Asatru mythology. Her magical apples are said to keep the gods young and prevent them from aging or dying. Idunn is associated with fertility. It was believed that eating her apples could lead to increased fertility in women.

Festivals and Celebrations

Asatru and Norse Paganism are ancient religions steeped in tradition dating back centuries. As part of these ancient traditions, various festivals and celebrations are associated with the religion honoring gods and goddesses and important events throughout the year. These festivities vary from region to region and provide an opportunity to reconnect with the old ways and celebrate spirituality within the community.

The Viking Age calendar was divided into two distinct seasons, summer (light) half and winter (dark) half. In modern times, March 20th marks the beginning of summer, and October 31st marks its end. Each season is symbolically linked to certain deities honored through celebration at each season's change. Summer is associated with the Norse gods Freyr and Freyja, while winter is associated with Odin and Ullr.

One of the most important Asatru festivals is called Ostara, which takes place at the spring equinox (March 20th). This ancient festival celebrates the rebirth of nature after a long winter and symbolizes renewal. It was traditionally celebrated by offering gifts to the gods, feasting, and singing songs in their honor. The festival is closely associated with Easter as both share similar themes, such as fertility and new beginnings.

The summer solstice (June 21st) or Midsummer's Day marks another important event on the calendar for Norse Paganism followers. This celebration honors Freyja, who presides over fertility and the beginning of summer. It is believed that on this day, the Sun god, Baldur, rises from the dead to bring light and life back into the world. People celebrate Midsummer's Day by gathering for bonfires, feasting, and dancing.

Lammas (August 1st) marks the harvest season and celebrates Freyr, who presides over wealth and abundance. This festival is a time to give thanks for all that was harvested during the year and for people to share in its bounty. Lammas is known as Loaf Mass because it was traditionally celebrated by offering bread made from grain from the harvest to Freyr.

The winter solstice (December 21st) is another important festival marking the year's longest night. This day is associated with Odin, who presides over death, wisdom, magic, and runes. People celebrate this day by giving offerings to Odin and lighting candles in his honor. The Yule log is traditionally burned, bringing warmth and light into homes during the long winter months.

Walpurgis Night (April 30th) celebrates Ullr, the god of hunting, skiing, and archery, and his divine wife, Freya. This celebration is not in traditional Viking calendars but has become one of the most popular festivals among modern-day Norse Paganism followers. It was originally celebrated by lighting bonfires in honor of Ullr and Freya and making offerings to them. Today, it is celebrated more as an opportunity for people to get together for feasting and merrymaking.

The festivals associated with Asatru and Norse Paganism allow people to connect with their ancient spiritual roots while celebrating the seasons' changes. They are a time for honoring gods and goddesses, giving thanks, sharing food, and enjoying fellowship within the community. These festivities help keep these ancient traditions alive in modern times and ensure that the old ways will never be forgotten.

Rituals

Blot

The Blot ritual is one of the most important rituals in Asatru. It consists of offering sacrifices to the gods or goddesses and hallowing them with ale, mead, and other libations. The ritual's purpose is for practitioners to honor the gods and goddesses and ask for their blessings in return. It is a way to thank the gods and goddesses for all they have done and given to the practitioner.

You need an altar, a chalice or other vessel for libation, an offering like food or drink (usually mead or ale), runes, incense, candles, and something to represent each god or goddess honored to perform this ritual. If a group is performing the ritual, it's best to each bring something representing each god or goddess being honored so they can all be acknowledged during the ceremony.

Instructions:
1. Set up your altar with items, such as offerings and representations of each god and goddess being honored.
2. Light candles and incense before saying a short prayer invoking all of the gods and goddesses being honored.
3. Pass around your chalice filled with mead or ale so that everyone can take part in hallowing it.

4. Once everyone has taken part in hallowing your offerings, take turns speaking words of gratitude for whatever each god and goddess has done for you
5. Pour your libation on the ground near your altar, representing their acceptance of your offerings.
6. When finished speaking words of thanksgiving and pouring out your libations, close your invocation with another short prayer thanking them again
7. Close down your ritual space.

Sumbel

Sumbel is a ritual with roots in the ancient Asatru religion. It is practiced today by modern adherents and as a regular part of a ceremony or at special events. The word Sumbel comes from the Old English term "drinking together." It is an important part of many gatherings and celebrations in Asatru.

The Sumbel ritual aims to honor the gods, ancestors, and other spirits and celebrate life's milestones. During the ritual, participants pledge or make oaths to each other and share words of encouragement. It strengthens bonds between family members and friends while demonstrating respect for each other's beliefs. Additionally, participants are encouraged to reflect on their actions and how they impact those around them.

The structure of the ritual is similar to a toast-making ceremony. However, the content varies depending on the event being celebrated or honored. Generally, Sumbel rituals involve drinking mead (or juice if mead isn't available) from a horn or cup known as "the blessed cup," passed from one person to another clockwise. Each time someone takes a sip from the cup, they honor someone else in attendance with kind words or symbolism, like pouring some drink out onto the grass or the earth outside to honor land spirits. Once everyone has had their turn with the blessed cup, there is usually laughter and joyous celebration accompanied by singing and folk dancing.

Seiðr

Seiðr is an Old Norse magical ritual widely practiced in pre-Christian Scandinavia. It is believed to have been used for various purposes, such as healing, divination, protection, and even cursing. It was most commonly performed by shamans or chieftains believed to be in touch with the gods and could influence events through their magic. The ritual usually involved chanting or singing, drumming on a hide, ecstatic dancing, and trances. The shaman would call upon otherworldly powers, such as elves and dwarves, to help them accomplish their tasks.

To perform a Seiðr ritual in the Asatru tradition creating the right environment for a successful magical event is necessary.

Instructions:
1. You need a sacred place where you can perform the ritual without any disturbances from outside sources. It can be inside or outside your home.
2. Prepare yourself mentally and spiritually for the ritual, like meditating beforehand, so that your mind is clear and open for what will happen during the ritual.
3. Once these steps have been taken, it is time to set up the space for the ritual. The space should face northwards toward Asgard (the realm of the gods).
4. A fire should be burning. At least two fires with candles placed around them.
5. Light some incense. It must be lit before chanting (usually with herbs like Juniper).
6. The chanting should consist of mantras associated with certain gods or spirits. Each god and spirit has its particular sound and will summon its energy into your circle.
7. Chanting can usually last up to ten minutes or more, depending on the depth of your trance.
8. When the chanting is completed, create a shield with runes. These runes should be chosen according to what you want to achieve with your Seiðr ritual, whether answers from the gods about something specific or casting a spell on someone.
9. End your ritual by thanking all of those who participated.
10. Close your sacred space until the next time.

Knowing how and why to do a seiðr ritual is important. It is an offering or prayer to gods and spirits so that they will intervene on your behalf when guidance or assistance is required. This makes the seiðr ritual exceptionally special and powerful in Asatru tradition.

Chapter 4: Germanic Paganism

"Germanic" refers to a tribal collective of Indo-Europeans from the Iron Age who spoke the Germanic languages and settled in Germany, the British Isles, and Scandinavia. This chapter focuses on Germanic pagan cultures like the Icelanders, the Anglo-Saxons, the Danes, and more. Besides providing information regarding their pagan traditions, the chapter offers a historical overview of Germanic pagan tribes and their migrations.

The History of Germanic Pagans

While it's unclear when the Germanic tribes arrived in Northernmost Europe, by 750 BCE, they were commonly established in the territories of modern-day Denmark and southern Scandinavia. Their popularity expanded so much that 500 years later, they migrated toward central Europe. Their migrations caused conflict with the Celts, who were also expanding their cultural influence. However, the Celts were defeated by the Germanic tribes. Later, the population growth caused several tribes to invade each other's territory, while others migrated to Italy, Spain, and Gaul. In the 5th century AD, many tribes merged, forming tribes like Anglo-Saxons, the Danes, the Swedes, and others.

Germanic tribes had rituals similar to the Celts, such as sacrifice.'

These migrations, conflicts, and coexisting beliefs of the different Germanic tribes left their mark on their belief systems. Archaeological findings indicate that during the Roman Iron Age (before 400 AD), the Germanic tribes practiced similar spiritual rituals as the Celts. They had similarities in how they offered sacrifices to deities and conducted divination, and, like the Celts, they believed in forming a spiritual connection with nature. However, they had a unique tradition of burning their dead before burying them in the ground. Some traditions were still practiced in the Germanic Iron Age (from the beginning of the 5th century), but soon after, Germanic tribes were converted to Christianity. However, this was an earlier and less festivity-based form of Christianity, so many Germanic Pagan practices survived through oral traditions or written records. Records from the early middle ages show a widespread reverence toward the Old Norse deities, priests, and natural phenomena.

The Icelanders

The Icelanders were a small group of Germanic pagan people who arrived on the shores of Iceland at the end of the 9th century. They had and maintained very similar beliefs to their Germanic pagan ancestors. They venerated the same gods and worshiped ancestors and nature with the same fervor. Their belief system is one of the most preserved from the North Germanic pagan tribes. They were preserved by oral tradition and recorded in sagas and, even more famously, the Poetic Edda, one of the most widely known sources of Norse mythology.

The Anglo-Saxons

According to historical records, the Anglo-Saxons arrived on the shores of Great Britain at the end of the 5th century. They carried pagan beliefs very similar to Norse Paganism. However, their religion later diversified under the influence of separation from the rest of the pagan tribes and later the pressure from other religions. They worshiped Woden (Odin), the highest god of their Pantheon. According to Anglo-Saxon beliefs, Woden was the god of death, who guided the departed souls toward their path in the afterlife. Unlike other more grounded authority figures they worshiped, he was universally feared, like the gods Tiw (Thir) and Thu (Thor).

Besides the indications of natural-based worship places, Archeological findings suggest the Anglo-Saxons might have built pagan temples. There, they held rituals addressing their deities and offered sacrifices to them.

The Danes

The Danes were a Germanic tribe that arrived in southern Scandinavia around the middle of the 6th century. They spoke Proto-Norse, and later Old Norse, and had similar beliefs to the North Germanic tribes. Their religion is woven with elements of Norse Paganism, worshiping Thor, Odin, and Frey. Like many other Germanic pagan tribes, the Danes left behind other deities. However, they participated in ancestral worship and maintained many original customs even after converting to Christianity in the 10th century. For example, they used the same burial practices and practiced runic divination. Besides the traditional Germanic Christianity that appeared in the 10th century, the Danes were influenced by Arian beliefs (a much older version of Christian doctrine emanating from 3rd-century Egypt).

Key Points in the Germanic Pagan Belief System

Germanic Paganism is an umbrella term for several closely related pagan beliefs interlocked in one large system. Most of these beliefs and traditions stem from the Old Norse religion, but in the medieval period, these were heavily influenced by Christian theology. Like their ancestors, the Germanic pagan belief system is also polytheistic. Many religious practices of the Germanic tribes of North-Western Europe were lost. However, it is known that even before medieval times, Germanic Paganism was more about individual worship and family traditions than about the tribes having one organized religion. Still, their traditions had a consistent framework. They typically revolved around the deities and the cycle of life. It is believed that the ancient Germanic tribes had traditions around their belief in the underworld, continued life after death, a world of ancestors in the heavens, and reincarnation. Germanic mythology has several variations of the creation myth. According to the most famous one, there was nothing but a magic void in the beginning. Odin and his brothers created the Earth from it and later gave life to humankind from two lifeless tree trunks.

Most Important Gods and Goddesses

According to ancient Germanic pagan mythology, the Pantheon of gods comprises two tribes, Vanir and Aesir. It is believed that once these tribes realized neither side could win, they made peace.

The Aesir

Odin

Odin was the ruler of Aesir and the god of kings and Germanic noblemen. The common people, however, rarely turned to Odin for help, and he wasn't widely worshiped. In Germanic Paganism, Odin is known as the god of poetry. There are many stories about how Odin brought the sacred mead of poetry to the gods. According to one of these stories, the mead was created from the blood of a wise god, Kvasir, who was killed by dwarfs. Odin stole it and escaped with it in the shape of an eagle, carrying the mead in his crop.

Odin was also known for his propensity to incite fights among the warriors and turn them against each other to recruit heroes in Valhalla. The dead heroes would join him in the final battle against Ragnarök. Odin was also said to create powerful magic that could make dead men talk. He was a magician, a shapeshifter, and a powerful shaman, who could enter a trance and journey into other worlds. When he visited the dead, he was always accompanied by two ravens and two wolves. The birds were his messengers, informing him of happenings in the otherworld and the world of mortals.

In Germanic Paganism, Odin is portrayed as the god of the hanged. This belief stems from the Old Norse myth of Odin suspending himself on the Yggdrasill (the tree of life) to gain wisdom.

While Odin was often considered untrustworthy by the commoners, he was a sovereign deity. The descendants of the ancient Germanic tribes across England and Scandinavia regarded him as their uppermost divine ruler. Foundations of dynasties are still attributed to Odin, and for centuries, he was offered extraordinary sacrifices for his blessings. While he was typically presented with animal sacrifice, human sacrifice was not uncommon. However, the latter stems from Roman writers who magnified the gruesomeness of Germanic pagan practices to instill fear and misconceptions.

Thor

Thor was a widely worshiped deity. He was one of the last deities people turned to before the end of the pagan period in Germanic lands. Thor is Odin's son. His name is derived from the Germanic word for thunder. Myths describe Thor as the champion of the gods, raving about his victories over giants. His success is often attributed to his hammer, Mjölnir. He had adventures with other mythical creatures, like the cosmic serpent Jörmungand. This creature lived in the ocean surrounding the world. After pulling the monster out of the vast waters, Thor fails to kill it and is expected to face it again at Ragnarök.

Unlike his father, Thor is the god of the common Germanic pagan people. Places across England and eastern Scandinavia were named after him. He was worshiped as the god of thunder and was thought to bring rain and ensure a good harvest. Warriors were guided into battles by him and called on him to assist in their military enterprises.

Thursday (Donnerstag in German) is named after Thor, meaning Thor's day. Modern Germanic pagan practitioners still believe Thor travels in his chariot in the sky toward the east daily, and thunder is the sound of his chariot.

Balder

In Germanic mythology, Balder is another son of Odin. Unlike Thor, Balder is a much more patient god. He had prophetic powers and even foretold his own death. According to the lore, his mother made all creatures take an oath not to harm him. However, after the mistletoe refused to take the oath, Loki, the trickster god, tore it off, handing it to the blind god, Höd, who inadvertently used it to kill Balder. When the gods sent to retrieve Balder's soul from Hel, he couldn't be released because the goddess of death was not paid what she asked in return. According to her decree, everyone should have grieved Balder's death. Loki disguised himself as a giantess and refused to mourn Balder, so Balder had to remain dead.

According to the Danes, Balder wasn't an innocent deity whose death was supposed to be a mournful event. They believed him to be a vicious demigod. Balder and Höd were constantly fighting for the hand of Balder's wife, and Höd killed him in one of their many fights. Across later Germanic pagan beliefs, Balder was often described as a dying spring god. However, given that these depictions gave him Christ-like features, they might have been influenced by Christian beliefs.

Loki

Although Germanic pagans count Loki among the Aesir, he is considered an outsider to this tribe. His father was a giant, and probably his mother, too. Loki is the father of Jörmungand, the serpent surrounding the world. He fathered Hel, the goddess of death, and Fenrir, the wolf whose destiny is to be chained until Ragnarök. According to their beliefs, Loki is bound but will undoubtedly break his chains when Ragnarök comes. He will honor his father and his progeny by joining the giants in the battle against the gods.

While Loki was known to deceive the gods, he also helped them at times, particularly Odin and Thor. He is a trickster deity who can change shape at will. For example, in one tale, he was depicted fighting Heimdall in the form of a seal for a necklace. Another poem describes his adventure in Freyja's residence in the form of a fly. Across Germanic pagan beliefs, Loki represents a source of impulsive intelligence. Under his influence, a person can act with unpredictable maliciousness.

Minor Aesir

Minor deities in the ranks of the Aesir included Heimdall, Rigr, and Tyr. Forever at odds with Loki, Heimdall and the trickster god are bound the kill each other at Ragnarök. According to the lore, Heimdall was born from nine mothers, who were presumed sisters and probably giantesses. Heimdall lived at the edge of the Aesir world, guarding it against the giants. He has incredibly powerful hearing and can pick up on anything in either world.

Rigr can possibly be one of the faces of Heimdall but is also said to be the father of humankind. Rigr bore children with three females, who gave birth to the three different races according to German pagan beliefs.

Tyr was a prominent divine figure during the early days of Germanic Paganism but has almost been forgotten. He only had one hand because the wolf Fenrir removed the other. He is a brave god and is believed to be the son of Odin. Some sources claim that rather than being a deity, Tyr was fathered by a giant.

Frigg

Like her husband, Odin, Frigg is depicted in several ways in various Germanic sources. Some show her as the weeping and self-sacrificing mother of her children, including Balder. Others described her as a libertine who wasn't afraid to live passionately. The latter sources claim that her misconduct was responsible for the poor fame and the brief banishment of Odin from the divine Pantheon.

The Vanir

The Vanir were another group of Germanic pagan deities. Most were associated with health, fertility, and weight. Unlike the Aesir, the Vanir rarely participated in battles nor influenced the outcome of conflicts and wars as the Aesir did.

Freyr

The eastern Danes notably celebrated Freyr, the son of Njörd. They believed that Freyr regularly departed eastward, traveling on a giant wave with his chariot following him. According to the Germanic tribes inhabiting the modern-day territory of Sweden, Freyr traveled inside the chariot. He brought blessings of fertility and a good harvest to the barren lands that lay beforehand in this Northern European territory. According to an Icelandic saga, when people began to cultivate crops, Freyr appeared to watch over the field. Therefore, the fields became sacred.

One of the most epic adventures of Freyr was the conquest of Gerd, a giant maiden who later became his wife. There are several renditions of this myth. One claims that Gerd was taken to the otherworld, and to get to her, Freyr had to overcome the rules of life and death. According to another version, the maiden was held captive by winter, bringing frost giants, whom Feyr had to battle for her. The latter story became a nature-based fertility myth in which Freyr is the Sun god who frees Gedr, the ruler of the Earth. Once the Earth is freed in Spring by Freyr, nature becomes fertile after winter.

Several animals were sacred to Freyr, including the horse and the boar (known for its high fertility). The Danes had a similar deity called Frody, who was responsible for the land's prosperity. Since he was also carried in a chariot, some said he was Freyr under a different name. Freyr was believed to be the ancestor of the Yngling, the Swedish royal family.

Freyja

Freyja is Freyr's sister (and wife for a brief period) and the goddess of love, fertility, and beauty, indicating very similar responsibilities to her brother. According to the lore, she is often surrounded by fine items, including jewelry. One of her most famous pieces was the Brísingamen necklace, forged by dwarfs and later stolen by Loki. Loki and Heimdall famously fought over it. Freyja was said to be a faithful wife, often depicted weeping tears of gold when her husband was away. However, some sources claim that she was rather promiscuous. The latter probably stems from the tales of her practicing magic unknown to many - even between the gods. This was seiðr magic, which Odin used on a few selected deities. Similarly to Odin, she guided the souls of those who fell in battle.

The fertility goddess Freyja is associated with animals. It represents a controversial feature of a fertility goddess associated with the otherworld, which wasn't present outside Germanic pagan beliefs.

Due to Freya's dual nature, she is often symbolized by a wide range of items, including a dog and a snake (alluding to their connection to the otherworld) or fruit, the ultimate symbol of fertility. Some tribes had a similar goddess under different names, like the goddess Nehawho, worshiped by Germanic tribes in central Europe.

Festivals and Celebrations

In traditional pagan fashion, the Germanic tribes didn't like to confine their worship and ritual practices within walls. Across the Germanic pagan world, nature-based practices were widespread, with the most common places of worship being sacred groves and woodlands. Tribes in Scandinavia, England, and continental Europe held their rituals and ceremonies near trees and wells. When they built temples and similar closed worship sites, they did it near sacred trees and wells.

According to Roman sources, the early Germanic pagan tribes did not visualize their deities in human forms. Whatever items were used to represent the divinities, they were effigies denoting divine power rather than any form. Later, these symbols became anthropomorphic in nature.

Most common Germanic pagan practices were (mostly animal) sacrifices offered to gods and goddesses. During these sacrifices, the number nine was significant. They presented nine heads or other organs to the gods to appease them and placed the offering near or in a sacred grove where they left it for nine days. They believed anything they put near the grove became sacred.

They conducted sacrifices by sending items where no one could access them, like the bottom of a lake. Or, they would simply burn the sacrificial object for similar purposes. They held sacrificial festivals (one of the rare festivals celebrated in ancient Germania), which involved festive meals and libations. During these celebrations, large public offerings were made, often gathering one or more tribes, where sometimes wooden figures were sacrificed instead of people.

Another Germanic pagan tradition was the offering of weapons to the deities. Archeological findings suggest the tribes would often throw into a lake or sacrifice weapons rendered useless after a battle. Interestingly, weapons were always sacrificed separately from other sacrificial items. Besides their own useless weapons, the tribes often offered their defeated enemy's weapons to the gods. Most offerings were made to Odin as an expression of gratitude for his blessings that led the winning party to victory. The sacrifice affirmed the connection between Odin and his worshipers and ensured this short-tempered god always stayed on their side.

Burial ceremonies were widespread. They often burned and buried the departed and their possessions, including animals and enslaved people. Before their burial, the animals and enslaved people were treated with the same respect as their masters, often receiving the same food, drink, and other privileges. During the intensive migration periods, the burial ceremonies were held on the shore or on ships.

While unified festivals were rare among the Germanic pagans, those that existed revolved around the deities. They held a public celebration of the gods and goddesses on the days associated with them. The modern names of the days of the week originate from the deities the Germanic pagans associated with them. Publicly honoring the deities on their sacred days gave the people a sense of community and reaffirmed their connection to the divine. Some festivals and celebrations were in reverence to the seasons. Early on, the Germanic pagans celebrated seasons equivalent to winter, spring, and summer. However, later groups, like the Icelanders, held only winter and summer celebrations.

Blot Ritual

The blot ritual was common in different Germanic tribes and is practiced today. Traditionally the blot is offered to a deity on the days associated with them. You can make a blot to a different deity each day of the week. Here is an example of an offering to Thor:

Ingredients:
- A glass or bottle of a natural drink. You can use water, natural juices, or anything that doesn't contain artificial flavors.

Instructions:
1. Find a quiet space in nature before sundown. If you're doing the ritual on a Thursday, you'll start by facing east as Thor travels toward the east.
2. Hold the cup or bottle between the palms of your hands and move it toward your belly. Aim to hold it at the level of your belly button.
3. Visualize how your energy travels from your palms and belly toward the bottle or cup and the drink inside it.
4. Take a deep breath through your nose and slowly exhale, chanting the name of Thor (or another deity).
5. Now that the liquid has been charged with your essence, it's ready to be offered to the chosen deity.
6. Pour some of the liquid out, and raise it toward the sky, offering it to the deity.
7. Hold the cup or bottle with both hands, place it in front of your belly, and repeat the chanting nine times.
8. Now the liquid has been charged with the power of the deity you're holding the blot for.
9. Raise the drink once again toward the sky, acknowledge the deity's blessings, and drink from it.
10. Don't drink it all at once, but take small sips throughout the evening. This way, you'll feel the deity's power coursing through you, slowly enveloping you with protection and healing.

Finding Connection to Nature

Nature plays a pivotal role in Germanic pagan traditions. Finding your connection to nature's energies is a ritual of empowerment and a way to establish balance in your life. Spending time in nature or near an element of nature in the morning is a great reminder to take as you continue your day.

Instructions:

1. After waking up in the morning, pick up a charm, talisman, or representation of the deity or spirit you've felt connected to recently and carry it with you.
2. Make your coffee, tea, or breakfast, and find a piece of nature. If you can go outside in a garden or terrace, do it. If you can't go outside, open a window and sit beside it. Alternatively, you can sit beside a potted plant; this also represents nature.
3. Whichever option works for you, have your drink or breakfast doing it.
4. While you do, use nature's power to ground yourself and calm your mind.
5. When relaxed, take the charm, talisman, or whatever object you've picked up beforehand and meditate. You don't have to have a particular notion. Wanting a connection to nature and your spirituality is more than enough.
6. You can meditate for as long as you want, but 5 minutes is usually enough. The entire exercise (along with consuming your drink or meal) doesn't have to last longer than 15 minutes.
7. You will feel empowered and ready to take on the day's challenges.

Chapter 5: Slavic Paganism

This chapter introduces Slavic Paganism, referring to the beliefs and practices of the ancient Slavic people of Eastern Europe. While Slavs are usually subdivided into East, West, and South Slavs, the core beliefs and deities are much the same across all Slavic territories. Besides learning about the most prominent Slavic gods and goddesses, myths, and festivals, you will learn to master a beginner-friendly Slavic pagan ritual at the end of the chapter.

The Slavic Pagan Path and Its History

In a typical pagan fashion, Slavic beliefs and traditions were passed down orally, and the ancient religion was also heavily influenced by Christianity. Very few records of the old Slavic belief system exist. One of the few written sources that exist is the "Slavic Primary Chronicle," originating from the early 12th century. It compiles the religious beliefs of the Slavs, mainly those revolving around the two most prominent Slavic gods, Perun and Veles. According to this source, a peace treaty in the 10th century between the Eastern Slavs and the Byzantine Emperors resulted from the Slavs' desire to maintain the balance between the powers of the two deities.

Dazhbog, the Sun god.[5]

Some records indicate that in the 10th century, Eastern Slavs worshiped a distinct Pantheon of gods known as the Pantheon of Prince Vladimir. It included the deities Dazhbog, Hors, Stribog, Simargl, and Mokosh. Some are still celebrated today, but the traditions revolving around others have been lost.

While records about West Slavic pagans are more prolific than those depicting the Eastern Slavs' beliefs, these stem from the 12th century, when most Slavs converted to Christianity. Unfortunately, their customs were recorded by German priests who didn't speak Slavic languages. Consequently, many of the meanings behind the traditions were lost in translations. "Chronica Slavorum," a document created in the late 12th century, mentions Czrnobog, Zorya, and Perun, some of the most important gods to the Western Slavs. It also mentions several unnamed Slavic deities with multiple heads.

Statues of Slavic deities were discovered in many Slavic regions. These were tall stone monuments erected in higher places. Many statues have multiple faces, indicating that different deities had several aspects. Some sites contained several shrines dedicated to various aspects of the same deity. Other findings included a human-sized wooden statue with two heads, hinting that some cultures might have viewed the deities as people with supernatural abilities. Russian mythology experts agree that many archeological remains of the different ancient Slavic cultures and religions have common roots.

Key Points in the Slavic Pagan Belief System

Slavic mythology points to a polytheistic belief system. However, it emphasizes the worship of deities with several aspects. Many Slavic gods have several faces and personalities and could exhibit different powers. They're celebrated at altars or shrines, near or in nature. Slavic Paganism is a religion relying heavily on nature. Its followers aim to respect nature as much as possible, emphasizing the importance of using natural resources correctly.

Slavic pagan practitioners often use nature's power in rituals, spells, and ceremonies, representing it with air, earth, fire, and water. They also employ salt, which has cleansing properties and is often used to purify the self, the home, objects, or magical tools. They burn salt to get black salt, which has even more powerful cleansing properties because it is burned with healing flowers. Flowers, herbs, and spices represent another way Slavic pagans use nature's power in their practices.

For Slavic pagans, the Sun and the Moon are the most potent sources of protective and healing energies. Basking in the sunlight can provide the empowerment to face upcoming hurdles. Whereas gazing into the moonlight will cleanse a person's energy. Similarly, leaving objects under the Sun or Moon will charge them with their respective powers.

The Slavic pagans have several popular divination methods. One of the most widespread involves melting wax and pouring it into water. As the wax hardens in the water, it forms certain shapes, which are analyzed to determine what messages they can reveal about future outcomes.

The Most Important Gods and Goddesses

While it's unclear whether the Slavic pagans ever had a unified Pantheon of gods, they do have several deities that were and still are worshiped across several Slavic regions.

Perun

Perun, the god of thunder, watched over the sky and sent lighting. He was a god of war and had many similarities with the Norse gods Odin and Thor. Perun was associated with oak trees and active parts of nature and is often described as a heavily masculine entity.

According to a famous Slavic myth, in ancient times, a sacred oak tree was the home of all living creatures in this world. The tree's top branches symbolized heaven; its trunk and lower branches were reserved for the earth, while its roots represented the underworld. Perun resided on the top branches to see everything that happened in the world. In ancient times, Perun was typically honored in nature, and later devotees built temples and shrines for him. These were erected in higher places so the messages could reach Perun more easily.

Dzbog

Dzbog was the god of fortune and the governor of fire and rain. According to Slavic legends, he gave life to the crops in the fields at the beginning of time and every spring since. His name can be translated into abundance or "the giving god," implying that he can provide plentiful bounty and harvest. Dzbog was the patron of the hearth fire, another element allowing a home to be filled with something everyone needs: love and spiritual prosperity. Devotees made offerings to Dzbog by a burning fire, asking him to ensure they would always have fire to warm up during the colder months.

Veles

Veles was the infamous shapeshifter god. Unlike Perun, who only brought rain and lighting, Veles brought storms that did more damage than good. Due to the rivalry between these two deities, Veles was often said to use tricks to get close to Perun. For example, one tale describes him taking on the form of a serpent and slithering up the sacred oak tree to see what Perun was doing on the top branches. According to other legends, Veles stole Perun's bride and children and hid them in the underworld. In many aspects, Veles is very similar to Loki, the Norse Pagan trickster god. He is said to practice magic and sorcery to bring hurdles and mishaps into people's and gods' lives.

Belobog and Czernobog

Belobog and Czernobog represent the rules of opposite forces. The first was the god of light, while the other was the god of darkness. Some say they were not two deities but the two aspects of the same deity. The latter belief stems from the lack of evidence about Belobog or Czernobog being worshiped individually. While the origins of either deity are unknown, most Slavic Pagans agree that Czernobog (the black god) was a deity with dark propensities. He was probably cursed early in his life and became associated with death and misfortune. If people weren't careful enough to protect themselves, Czernobog could easily cause plenty of calamity in their life. In some legends, he is described as a demon, indicating the source of all things evil. On the other hand, Belobog was the total opposite. His name is translated as the white god and was often prayed to for blessings, guidance, and protection from evil, including Czernobog.

Lada

Lada was the goddess of love and beauty, associated with spring and fertility. She was the Slavic patron of matrimony and newlyweds. Lada was often summoned to weddings to bless the newlywed couples union. She had a twin brother Lado, who had similar associations and was also called upon to bless mortal unions. Other sources claim that Lada and Lado were two faces of the same entity, unified in the perfect balance of feminine and masculine energy. It allowed them to bring harmony to couples' lives. In some sources, Lada is given a motherly role. She is said to be nurturing toward those who follow and celebrate her. Lada is similar to the Norse goddess Freyja, who is also associated with love, beauty, and fertility.

Marzanna

Marzanna was the Slavic goddess of winter and death. She was responsible for the death of the earth during the winter months. However, she is believed to be dead with the soil, only to be revived again in the spring. Some tales claim she is reborn as Lada, while other myths affirm that Lada only takes over the rule over the earth in the spring. In several Slavic traditions, Marzanna is symbolized by an effigy, either burned or drowned during a ritual signifying the end of a life cycle and the beginning of the new one.

Mokosh

Mokosh was the fertility goddess and the protector of women. As a motherly figure, she watched over pregnant women and their children's birth and ensured their well-being as they raised their children. She is linked to domestic duties associated with women, including cooking, weaving, and spinning. Among the Eastern Slavs, Mokosh was often seen as a source of fertility. They made offerings to her and represented her with breast-shaped stones in rituals and ceremonies, presenting these at her altar. Other times, she is depicted with male reproductive organs because, as a fertility deity, she is also responsible for male fertility.

Svarog

Svarog was the fire deity, the god of the Sun, similar to Hephaestus in Greek mythology. He was associated with metalsmithing and metal forging. In Slavic mythology, Svarog was the creator of the world. Svarog sometimes worked alongside Perun, and the two deities are often blended into an all-mighty father god. According to the lore, Svarog created the world of mankind in his sleep. His dreams shaped the Earth and the world as everyone knows it. Some sources claim that Svarog continues to shape the world as he continues to sleep, and when he wakes up, the world will end.

Zorya

In Slavic mythology, Zorya is the goddess of dusk and dawn. She is associated with the Morning and Evening Star, indicating that she has at least two aspects. Her morning aspect (Zorya Utrennjaja) opens the gates of heaven at dawn. Her evening aspect (Zorya Vechernjaja) closes the same gates at dusk. According to a well-known legend, Zorya dies at midnight following the Sun's death. She is reborn again in the morning, just as the Sun is revived at dawn.

Festivals and Celebrations

The world of the Slavic pagans is cyclical, meaning all events repeat each year. They usually follow the changes in nature and the seasons. The major events were celebrated over a series of colorful festivities incorporating different rituals, offerings, and feasts.

By observing Slavic mythology, it's easy to understand the most notable dates of their calendar. The Slavic calendar is based on the lunar year. This year begins on the first day of March, similar to the traditional calendars of other ancient pagan cultures. Several well-known holidays in modern-age calendars are based on Slavic pagan customs. Halloween and Easter are two examples of how the widespread traditions of worshiping Slavic deities have turned into modern holidays.

Another example is the festivities held in the name of Veles. He was the god of the underworld and was celebrated among Slavic pagans on the last day of the year. Below are the most prominent Slavic holidays.

Koleda

Koleda is the celebration of the beginning of the Slavic pagan year. In ancient times, this was a New Year celebration that took place during the winter solstice in December. After Slavic Paganism fell under Christianity's influence, Koleda was unified with the Christmas holidays. However, the name of the festivity has remained Koleda among those who follow the Slavic pagan path and is often celebrated through ancestral customs. According to different Slavic myths, the holiday is either named after Kolyada, the god of winter, or Koliada, the goddess who revives the Sun every morning.

Koleda is a deeply spiritual festival. Many devotees use it to celebrate with rituals, spells, and ceremonies as spiritual cleansers. This tradition is tied to the role of spirits in the Salvic belief system. The primary purpose of Koleda celebrations is to ward off evil spirits and toxic energies from around the home and self and replace them with good spirits and positive vibes.

In ancient times, Slavic people dressed up as animals and dedicated prayers and songs to the good spirits, often inviting them through dance. Sometimes, people let aggression take over them and would get into fights. It was a ritual allowing one last opportunity for the bad spirits to control the body, after which they had to leave people's lives. Dressing up as animals was a way to honor Veles, the god of the underworld, animals, and forests. Simultaneously, Koleda is also dedicated to another deity, Perun, the god of thunder. The two gods represent two sides of the same coin. One brings destruction, while the other creates. They establish natural abundance, which must be honored.

Koleda is a time of bonding for the Slavic pagan communities. Food is often shared in the community during this time. Depending on the local customs, people gather to eat, talk, and light a fire. The children are charged with gathering wood and bringing food to community gatherings. While they are doing this, they sing Kolyadki songs, which speak about wishes for happiness, prosperity, and peace for everyone at the end of the year.

Komoeditsa

Komoeditsa is a spring holiday dedicated to the bear god. The celebration occurs in early March, at the spring equinox, when people offer food to this deity by leaving it in the forest. In ancient times, people presented the bear god with crepes with homemade jelly or jam to sweeten up this deity. While this food offering ritual is rarely practiced in modern times, its new version, Maslenitsa, is very popular. Due to Christian influences, Maslenitsa has been blended into the Western Christian Carnival and is celebrated around the same time. It's a week-long festival ending with a ceremony called Forgiveness Sunday. During this ceremony, family, friends, and community members gather to share a feast and ask each other for forgiveness. They might exchange presents, often giving small items the other likes to show their remorse for whatever wrong they've done to them during the year.

In some territories, Komoeditsa is dedicated to the goddess Lada and her bother Lado, the Slavic deities who gain most of their powers around the spring equinox. Their strength lies in their ability to blend male and female energies, symbolizing the fertility of nature and new life. Consequently, the holiday celebrates the revival of nature in spring.

Krasnaya Gorka

Another springtime festivity in Slavic pagan cultures is Krasnaya Gorka. This festival allows young people to meet, share a conversation, get to know each other, possibly fall in love, and find their future spouses. While the festival lasts for several days, at the culmination, young maidens and men dress up, meet, dance together, and sing songs about love and happiness. In some regions, it is said that if a young single person stays at home during Krasnaya Gorka, they will remain single for the rest of their lives.

In other regions, the young folks are encouraged to paint eggs in yellow or green and share them. Besides bringing people together, this ritual honors the ancestors. Traditionally, young people make cakes and crepes. However, before that, they would exchange eggs and oil, which helped them remember and share their ancestors' wisdom.

Kupala

Kupala, known as Kupala night or summer solstice, is a summer holiday, traditionally celebrated in mid-June, on the shortest night of the calendar year. During these festivities, people gathered to sing cheerful songs, prank each other, and tell jokes. According to Slavic traditions, women were the most fertile on Kupala night, and many couples used it to conceive healthy children. Traditionally, it was believed that the night or the day before and after Kupala night increased the chances of a healthy birth.

Besides singing and dancing, people used water to symbolize their wishes for fertility and cleaning. Women who wanted to conceive would bathe in magically charged water to boost their feminine energy. Young maidens would decorate their hair with fresh flowers during the day, and when the night came, they took off their adornments and threw them into the river. The flowers thrown into the water represented a desire for a romantic relationship and marriage. If the flowers floated on the water's surface, the girl's wishes for marriage were granted. However, if the flowers sunk, no relationship or wedding would follow. Boys would enter the water, attempting to rescue the flowers and spark the interest of the maiden whose flowers they caught. In some regions, Kupala worship involves walking to the forest at twilight to find a fern flower, which was said to have magical properties and blooms only on this night. In other places, Kupala is simply celebrated by community members gathering beside a large log fire, singing, dancing, and jumping through the fire.

The Festival of Perun

The Festival of Perun is celebrated at the end of the summer. For the Slavic pagans, it is a way of greeting the new season and mourning the previous one. It's said that around this time of the year, powers in nature shift from feminine to masculine.

People celebrate the festival of Perun by offering and sacrificing to this deity. They know he was the power to keep nature favorable during autumn, so it's crucial to keep him appeased. The festivities often include lighting a sacred bonfire and wearing protective amulets, which were charged with positive energy beforehand. In ancient times, men would later wear these amulets when in battle. During the festival, warriors would show off their warfare skills. At the end of the festivities, men reenacted a fight between Perun and Veles, with the former being the victor.

The Festival of Mokosh

This festival marks the autumn equinox in Slavonic religions. It represents the beginning of the harvesting season and is celebrated with the Harvest festival (known as Rodogosch or Tausen). The festival culminates with a ritual dedicated to Mokosh, the goddess of the Earth.

Mokosh has often represented wet Earth, indicating her feminine energy. Devotees would light a fire in the hearth or, in modern times, a candle to honor the goddess. This goddess can be represented by a spinning wheel during rituals and ceremonies performed in her honor during the festival.

At the festival, women often ask Mokosh to help protect their families and keep them together and nurtured with positive energy. The celebration of Mokosh has decreased in popularity as the Slavic culture became more patriarchal. Nevertheless, there are still regions where she is celebrated through the old customs.

A Ritual to Connect with Nature

Since Slavic Paganism is a nature-based religion, the followers often perform rituals to enhance their connection to nature. The following easy-to-do rite can be conducted whenever you want to bring yourself closer to nature to obtain its blessings, including fertility and revival. It's recommended to perform this ritual on a sunny day in a place with plenty of sunlight, as the Sun is crucial in nature's fertility.

Ingredients:
- The representation of the four elements of nature, air, fire, earth, and water (you can use a candle for the fire)
- The representation of a fifth element, salt
- A representation of a natural being, for example, a plant or a small animal
- A representation of a deity (if you are working with one)
- Natural incense (like tree sap)
- Sunlight, or, alternatively, the representation of the Sun

Instructions:
1. Find a quiet space for your ritual, preferably near a window on a sunny day. If you have an altar, perform it there. Alternatively, go to a natural clearing and perform the ritual directly under the Sun. This way, you only need to carry a few ingredients to the ritual place (as some will already be there).
2. Gather your supplies and place them in front of you. The four elements should be placed at the four corners of the space in

front of you, while the fifth should be set in the middle.
3. Light the candle and place the plant or animal in front of you.
4. Take a deep breath and focus on your intention. Feel free to do it now if you call on a deity to empower your connection with nature.
5. When you're ready, address nature with the following words:

"Sacred nature, I respect and worship you.

You center and ground me, and I wish to remain close to you.

Please bless me with plentiful, and I will forever be thankful for your gifts."

6. Look up towards the Sun, and feel how it helps you re-form your connection to nature. Feel how you are revitalized and ready to take on life's challenges.
7. Later, you might even get inspired to be more productive or fertile in different areas of life.

Chapter 6: Greek Polytheism

Greek polytheism, often referred to as Hellenism, encompasses a wide range of beliefs and practices. At its heart, Hellenic polytheism comprises multiple spiritual paths arising from Greece's vibrant and complex ancient mythology. This polytheistic religion honors a diverse Pantheon of gods and goddesses, each with unique personalities, stories, and powers. Practitioners seeking to revive the ancient Greek religious practices into a modern pagan religion are known as Hellenes, Hellenic Reconstructionists, or Hellenic pagans. Conversely, other practitioners claim to have inherited the original ancient traditions passed down through the ages. Regardless of your path, Greek polytheism is a journey of discovery and a chance to explore the rich cultural heritage spanning thousands of years.

Greek gods and goddesses.[6]

Many people compare the Hellenistic belief system with Paganism. While the word "*pagan*" has historically been used to describe any non-Abrahamic religion, Hellenism is very much an umbrella term. The comparison of Hellenism with Paganism depends on how a person defines "Paganism." For instance, if you consider Paganism to be referring to non-Abrahamic faith, then yes, Hellenism does fall under the umbrella of pagan religions. However, if you define Paganism as the modern-day goddess-worshiping, Earth-based religion, Greek polytheism would not fit this description. Hellenic polytheism is more focused on the ancient Greek gods and goddesses.

Moreover, some Hellenes take issue with being labeled as pagans since many people assume all pagans are Wiccans, which is not the case for Hellenes. Some scholars argue that the term "pagan" was never even used by the Greeks themselves to describe their religions. This theory suggests that the origins of the word "pagan" comes from a Latin word, translated to "rustic" or "of the countryside," and was originally used by early Christians to refer to non-Christians. Outside society's mainstream, it was never used in Greece. More so because worship in ancient Greece was decentralized, and each city had its own cult and traditions. Therefore, the Greeks didn't consider themselves a unified entity like the Romans.

So, while Greek polytheism shares many similarities with Paganism, particularly its modern revival, people should be aware of the distinctions between these two belief systems. Hellenism is a rich and complex religion encompassing many aspects of Greek philosophy, religion, and social life. It emerged in ancient Greece during the classical period and profoundly influenced the development of Western civilization. This chapter comprehensively explains the Hellenistic belief system, including its historical development, customs, and practices. From its origins to modern-day celebrations, you will discover all aspects of Greek polytheism.

How History Shaped the Greek Belief System

Ancient Greece is known as the cradle of Western civilization, but how did this come about? How did the polytheistic belief system come into existence? What were the factors that shaped Hellenism and Greek mythology? The roots of the Greek belief system can be traced back to prehistoric times when the locals believed in numerous spirits and deities associated with nature. With time, cultural influences, and historical events, this belief system further developed into the complex Pantheon of gods we know today.

One of the most important factors was the influence of neighboring cultures. The Greeks were exposed to many religions and mythologies from other civilizations, including Egypt, Mesopotamia, and the Near East. They adopted and adapted many of these stories and beliefs, incorporating them into their religion. Each civilization contributed its unique elements to the development of Greek mythology and religion:

1. Egyptian Influence

The Greeks were fascinated by Egyptian religion and mythology, which had a complex Pantheon of gods and goddesses associated with specific natural phenomena and animals. The Greeks were particularly interested in the god Thoth, associated with knowledge and writing. Over time, they identified Thoth with their god Hermes, who became known as the messenger of the gods and the patron of travelers and merchants. It led to the development of Hermeticism, a spiritual tradition that combined elements of Greek and Egyptian religion and philosophy.

2. Mesopotamian Influence

The Babylonian creation myth of the god Marduk slaying the primordial dragon Tiamat and creating the world from her body was particularly influential on the Greek creation myth. In Greek mythology, Zeus and his siblings overthrow their father, the Titan Cronus, and establish themselves as the rulers of the universe. The Mesopotamian myth also influenced the story of the Greek hero Perseus, who slays the monster Medusa and uses her head as a weapon.

3. Near Eastern Influence

The Near East was also a major cultural influence on the Greeks, with the ancient city of Ugarit being a major center of trade and culture in the eastern Mediterranean. The Ugaritic Pantheon of gods and goddesses, including Baal, the god of storms and fertility, and Anat, the goddess of war and hunting, particularly influenced the Greeks. Many of the stories and attributes of these gods and goddesses were adapted and incorporated into the Greek Pantheon. For example, the goddess Athena, who was associated with war and wisdom, could have been influenced by the Near Eastern goddess Anath.

The polytheistic belief system of ancient Greece was influenced by neighboring cultures and shaped by the writings and works of Greek poets, playwrights, and philosophers. Here are some ways these individuals contributed to the development of Greek polytheism:

4. Hesiod and Homer

Hesiod and Homer were two of the earliest and most influential Greek poets. They wrote epic poems featuring gods and goddesses as major characters. Hesiod's "Theogony" and Homer's "Iliad" and "Odyssey" provided the Greeks with a foundation for their understanding of the gods and their relationships with each other and with mortals. Hesiod's "Theogony," in particular, details the world's creation and the gods' genealogy, an established hierarchy of deities, and helped define their roles and characteristics.

5. Greek Tragedy

Greek tragedy, which emerged in the 5th century BCE, was a major cultural force contributing to the development of Greek polytheism. Tragedy often featured stories about the gods and their relationships with mortals. It explored themes of fate, divine justice, and the limitations of human understanding. Playwrights such as Aeschylus, Sophocles, and Euripides used their plays to explore complex questions about the nature of the gods and their relationship with humanity. For example, in Sophocles' "Antigone," the heroine defies the city's laws to honor the divine law, leading to a conflict between the state's authority and the god's authority.

6. Greek Philosophy

Greek philosophy emerged in the 6th century BCE and contributed to the development of Greek polytheism. Philosophers like Plato and Aristotle used their works to explore the nature of the gods and their relationship with the world. For example, Plato's concept of the *Forms* suggested that the gods represented reality's highest and most perfect form. On the other hand, Aristotle argued that the gods were the unmoved movers of the universe, responsible for setting the world in motion but not actively intervening in human affairs.

The Greeks also believed in the concept of fate, which was closely tied to their understanding of the gods. They believed the gods controlled the events of the world and humans were subject to their whims. This idea was reinforced by the oracles revered throughout Greece as sources of divine wisdom and guidance.

Greek Polytheism and Spirituality

As you know by now, Hellenism is based on the worship of a Pantheon of gods and goddesses. At the core of Hellenic belief is the idea that everything in the world is interconnected. It is expressed through the concept of cosmos - referring to the order and harmony of the universe. The gods are believed to play an important role in maintaining this order, and their worship is a way of maintaining the balance between the natural world and human society.

The gods are a central part of Hellenic belief and practice. Each god or goddess is associated with a specific aspect of the natural world, like the sky, the sea, or the Earth. They are associated with virtues such as wisdom, courage, or beauty. Hellenic practitioners often develop personal relationships with the gods through prayer, meditation, and offerings. The gods are not seen as omniscient or omnipotent but are believed to have their own personalities, desires, and areas of influence.

Myths and legends are an essential part of the Hellenic tradition, woven into the very fabric of Hellenic culture. They are not just stories but repositories of wisdom, knowledge, and insight into the universe's workings. Through these myths and legends, Hellenic practitioners connect with the gods, understand the natural world's mysteries, and gain a deeper appreciation of their place in the cosmos.

Storytelling is vital to Hellenic practice, with many rituals and ceremonies incorporating myths and legends. These stories are often ritualized, with the storyteller acting as a conduit between the gods and the listeners. Through the power of storytelling, Hellenic practitioners can connect with the divine, gain insight into their lives, and strengthen the bonds with their community. One myth that shaped the belief system of Hellenism was Hesiod's Cosmogony.

Hesiod's Cosmogony is a creation myth explaining the universe's origins and the birth of the gods. It is a tale that has captured peoples' imaginations for centuries and continues to influence today's Hellenism belief system. Here's how it goes:

In the beginning, there was Chaos, a formless and empty void. From Chaos emerged two primal beings: Gaia, the Earth, and her firstborn, Uranus (known as Ouranos), the "starry heaven." Gaia had many children, including the Titans, who were the first gods. The Titans included powerful figures like Cronus, Rhea, and Oceanus.

However, Uranus was a cruel and tyrannical father, and his children were unhappy with him. Cronus, the youngest of the Titans, eventually rebelled against his father and overthrew him with the help of his mother, Gaia. After becoming the new ruler of the gods, Cronus became even more tyrannical than Uranus. He swallowed his children to prevent them from challenging him.

However, one of Cronus' children, Zeus, was spared from this fate. He grew up in secret and eventually overthrew his father, becoming the king of the gods. With the help of his siblings, the Olympians, Zeus defeated the Titans and became the undisputed ruler of the cosmos."

The story of Hesiod's Cosmogony provides a fascinating explanation for the universe's origins and is crucial in shaping the Hellenism belief system. The myth teaches the importance of order, balance, and harmony in the world. As the personification of these ideals, the gods serve as guides for mortals to follow in their daily lives.

Gods and Goddesses

Each god and goddess in Greek mythology had a unique role and attribute reflecting different aspects of the human experience. Together, they formed a complex and interconnected Pantheon to explain natural phenomena, human emotions, and the complexities of human relationships.

1. Zeus

Zeus was the king of the gods and the god of the sky and thunder. He was known for his power, strength, and wisdom. He was often depicted as a strong, muscular man with a beard, holding a lightning bolt. He was married to his sister, Hera, who was one of the twelve Olympian gods. Zeus was known for his numerous affairs and had many children with mortal and immortal women. He was known for his role in enforcing justice and maintaining order in the world.

2. Hera

Hera was the queen of the gods and the goddess of marriage, childbirth, and family. She was often depicted as a beautiful woman wearing a crown or headdress, holding a lotus flower or a scepter. She was fiercely loyal to her husband, Zeus, but was known for her jealousy toward his numerous affairs. She was a protector of women and children and was associated with the domestic realm. Her children included Hephaestus, the god of fire and craftsmanship, and Ares, the god of war.

3. Poseidon

Poseidon was the god of the sea, earthquakes, and horses. He was often depicted as a muscular man with a trident, riding a chariot pulled by horses. He was known for his temper and was often associated with destruction and creation. He was one of the three brothers who divided the world among themselves, with Zeus receiving the sky, Hades receiving the underworld, and Poseidon receiving the sea.

4. Demeter

Demeter was the goddess of agriculture and fertility. She was often depicted as a mature woman, carrying a sheaf of wheat or a cornucopia. She was Zeus' sister and the mother of Persephone, who was abducted by Hades and taken to the underworld. Demeter's grief at the loss of her daughter was said to have caused the change of seasons, with the barren winter months representing the time when Persephone was in the underworld.

5. Athena

Athena was the goddess of wisdom, strategy, and warfare. She was often depicted as a strong, beautiful woman wearing a helmet and carrying a shield and spear. She was born fully grown and armored from her father's head, Zeus. She was a virgin goddess associated with the arts, sciences, civic duty, and justice.

6. Apollo

Apollo was the god of music, poetry, prophecy, and healing. He was the son of Zeus and Leto and the twin brother of Artemis. He was known for his musical skills and was often depicted with a lyre or a bow and arrows. Apollo was associated with the Sun and was believed to drive his chariot across the sky daily. He was often consulted as an oracle at the temple of Delphi and believed to have the power to heal.

7. Artemis

Artemis was the goddess of the hunt, the wilderness, childbirth, and virginity. She was the daughter of Zeus and Leto and the twin sister of Apollo. Artemis was often depicted with a bow and arrows and was known for her skill as a hunter. She was associated with the Moon and was believed to help women during childbirth. Artemis was often revered as a protector of young women and a champion of virginity.

8. Demeter

Demeter was the goddess of agriculture, fertility, and the harvest. She was the daughter of Cronus and Rhea and the sister of Zeus. Demeter was often depicted with a sheaf of wheat or corn. She was revered as a protector of farmers and those who worked the land. She was associated with the seasons and believed to have the power to bring about the seasons' changes.

9. Dionysus

Dionysus was the god of wine, fertility, and theater. He was the son of Zeus and Semele and was often depicted holding a wine cup and surrounded by revelers. Dionysus was associated with the wild and was often worshiped in rituals that involved wine and ecstatic dancing. He was known for his ability to inspire creativity and was revered as a patron of the arts.

10. Hades

Hades was the god of the underworld and the dead. He was the son of Cronus and Rhea and the brother of Zeus and Poseidon. Hades ruled over the dead and was often depicted as a dark and foreboding figure. He was associated with wealth and riches, as the underground minerals were believed to be his domain. Mortals feared Hades, as death was seen as a final and irreversible separation from the world of the living.

11. Hephaestus

Hephaestus was the Greek god of fire, metalworking, and craftsmanship. He was the son of Zeus and Hera. Hephaestus was known for his exceptional skill in crafting weapons, armor, and other objects made of metal. Despite his important role in Greek mythology, he was often portrayed as physically unattractive, with a limp or deformed leg. According to stories, his mother cast him out of Olympus because of his appearance. He landed on Lemnos Island, where he set up his forge. Despite his physical limitations, Hephaestus was highly respected by the other gods for his skill and creativity. He was said to have crafted many of the most famous weapons and artifacts in Greek mythology, including the lightning bolts wielded by Zeus, the shield of Achilles, and the chariot of the Sun.

12. Hermes

Hermes was one of the twelve Olympian gods in Greek mythology. He was the son of Zeus and the Pleiad Maia and was known as the messenger of the gods. Hermes was a multifaceted god associated with many responsibilities, including commerce, thieves, travelers, athletes, and diplomacy. He was typically depicted as a youthful and athletic figure, often wearing a broad-brimmed hat and carrying a caduceus, a winged staff with two snakes wrapped around it. He was known for his speed and agility and was often called upon by the other gods to deliver messages or perform tasks. In addition to his role as a messenger, Hermes was the god of thieves and commerce. He was believed to be the protector of merchants and travelers and was associated with the boundaries between different places and realms.

Festivals and Celebrations

The Hellenic calendar was filled with numerous celebrations and rituals honoring the gods and goddesses of Greek mythology. These events served as religious observances and important social and cultural occasions that united communities.

One of the most well-known celebrations was the Olympic Games, held every four years in honor of Zeus. The games were a time for athletic competition and included events such as running, jumping, and wrestling. The winners were celebrated as heroes, and the games were a way to promote unity and peace among the city-states of ancient Greece.

Another important ritual was the Eleusinian Mysteries, held in honor of the goddess Demeter and her daughter Persephone. The mysteries were secret rituals only open to those who had been initiated into the cult of Demeter. The rituals were said to reveal the secrets of life, death, and the afterlife. They were believed to bring spiritual purification and enlightenment to those who participated.

The Dionysian festivals, held in honor of the god Dionysus, were another important event in the Hellenic calendar. These festivals were marked by wild and raucous music, dance, and feasting celebrations. The followers of Dionysus believed that by engaging in these ecstatic rituals, they could experience divine communion with the god and achieve a state of transcendence and spiritual liberation.

In addition to the traditional celebrations and rituals, modern-day festivals and events are inspired by Hellenic polytheism. These events are often organized by modern-day Hellenic communities and serve to honor the gods and goddesses of Greek mythology. One event is the Hellenic Revival Festival, which occurs in Greece annually. This festival features music, dance, and theater performances celebrating the Hellenic heritage of Greece and pays tribute to the ancient gods and goddesses.

Hellenic Ritual

Hellenism places great importance on the practice of rituals and ceremonies as ways of honoring the gods and maintaining a connection with the divine. These rituals often involve offering sacrifices, including food, drink, or animals. Temples and other sacred sites are important to Hellenic practitioners and where the gods can be contacted and worshiped. These rituals and offerings help reinforce the interconnectedness of the natural world and the relationship between humans and the gods.

One simple Hellenic ritual you can perform in your space is the Libation Ritual. This ritual involves pouring a small amount of wine, olive oil, or honey as an offering to the gods and goddesses.

Materials:
- A small bowl or cup for the libation
- Wine, olive oil, or honey
- A candle or incense for lighting
- Any offerings or symbols you would like to include, such as flowers, herbs, or statues of the gods and goddesses

Preparation:
- Set up a sacred space in your home or outdoor area, using symbols or objects meaningful to you.
- Light the candle or incense to create a peaceful and focused atmosphere.
- Choose which deity or deities you want to honor and prepare a small offering of wine, olive oil, or honey.

Ritual:
1. Stand before your altar or sacred space and take a deep breath, centering yourself in the present moment.
2. Light the candle or incense, and offer a prayer or invocation to the gods and goddesses, inviting their presence and blessing on your ritual.

3. Pour a small amount of the libation into the bowl or cup, and speak a few words of gratitude or intention to the deity you are honoring.
4. Raise the bowl or cup in your hands, and offer the libation as an offering to the deity. As you pour the liquid, you can say a prayer, chant a hymn, or simply offer your thoughts and intentions.
5. After the libation is poured, offer other offerings or symbols, such as flowers, herbs, or incense, and meditate or reflect on your connection to the deity and its teachings.
6. When you are ready, extinguish the candle or incense, and give thanks to the deity for their presence and blessings.

Safety and ethical considerations:
- Always be respectful and mindful when performing any spiritual practice.
- Use caution when working with candles or incense, and ensure they are not left unattended.
- Use only a small amount of alcohol if choosing wine for the libation, and avoid drinking excess alcohol during the ritual.

Greek Polytheism and Spirituality offer a unique and compelling view of the world that has influenced countless cultures throughout history. From the complex relationships between the gods and goddesses to the importance of music, dance, and feasting, this belief system offers a rich and diverse array of traditions that continue to inspire today. Whether you are an adherent of Paganism or merely interested in exploring new spiritual practices, the rituals and celebrations of Hellenism offer a powerful way to connect with the divine and find meaning in your life.

Chapter 7: Wicca: A Neopagan View

Paganism has been around for centuries, encompassing diverse spiritual practices and beliefs honoring the natural world and its cycles. However, it is hard not to immediately think of Wicca when you think of modern Paganism. Wicca emerged in the early 1950s as a new form of Paganism, drawing inspiration from ancient pagan practices and beliefs. Despite being relatively young compared to other pagan paths, Wicca has grown in popularity over the years and is a prominent and influential spirituality in modern times.

But what is Wicca? How does it differ from other forms of neopaganism? As you explore the world of Wicca and modern neopaganism, you will uncover a vibrant and diverse spiritual landscape honoring nature's sacredness and life's cycles. In particular, Wicca draws upon ancient pagan and magical practices while incorporating newer beliefs and ideas. From the Wiccan Rede to the various traditions and festivals, the Wiccan path is intriguing and complex. While often used interchangeably, not all neopagans are Wiccans, and vice versa. So, dive into the nuances and differences between Wicca and neopaganism, and discover what makes each path unique.

Wiccan traditions and spells honor nature.[7]

Origins of Wicca and Neopaganism

Wicca and neopaganism have their roots in ancient pagan practices, which were widespread throughout Europe before the spread of Christianity. The rise of Christianity led to the suppression and persecution of Paganism, but the beliefs and practices survived and continued to evolve in secret. In the early 20th century, interest in Paganism resurged, particularly with the growth of the occult and esoteric movements. In the 1950s, Gerald Gardner, an Englishman initiated into a coven of witches, publicly promoted Wicca as a new form of Paganism. It marked the birth of Wicca as a distinct spiritual path, although it drew heavily on ancient pagan beliefs and practices.

On the other hand, neopaganism refers to a broader umbrella of modern pagan paths that draw inspiration from various ancient traditions. It includes traditions such as Druidry, Asatru, and Hellenismos. Neopaganism emerged in the 1960s and 1970s. It is characterized by a strong focus on ecological and environmental concerns and a rejection of patriarchy and other hierarchical structures.

Comparison between Wicca and Neopaganism

Wicca is often associated with neopaganism. However, it is important to understand that they are not synonymous. While all Wiccans are neopagans to some degree, not all neopagans are Wiccans. Wicca is a specific neopaganism tradition with its own beliefs, practices, and rituals.

One of the key differences between Wicca and other neopagan traditions is the emphasis on witchcraft and magic. While many neopagan traditions incorporate magical practices, Wicca strongly emphasizes magic as a central aspect of its practice. Another difference is their use of covens. While some neopagan traditions practice in groups, Wicca is known for using covens typically led by a high priestess or priest.

The Wiccan Belief System

Wicca is a modern pagan religion with roots in ancient pagan practices. It is characterized by its reverence for nature, belief in a divine feminine and masculine figure, and use of magic and ritual. Here are some key points in the Wiccan belief system:

- **Polytheism:** Wiccans believe in the existence of multiple gods and goddesses, each with their distinct personalities and areas of influence. These deities are often associated with natural elements and forces like the Sun, Moon, and Earth.
- **Divine polarity**: Wiccans believe in the concept of divine polarity, which posits that the universe is made up of two complementary forces, the feminine and the masculine. These forces are often represented by a goddess and a god, respectively.
- **Reverence for nature:** Wiccans believe in the inherent sacredness of nature and seek to live in harmony with the natural world. They often celebrate the changing seasons and cycles of the Moon through ritual and ceremony.
- **The power of intention**: Wiccans believe that thoughts and intentions have the power to shape the world. It is often expressed through magic and rituals.

The Wiccan Rede and Its Importance

The Wiccan Rede is a statement of ethics central to the Wiccan belief system. It states, "An it harm none, do what ye will," meaning as long as your actions do not cause harm to others, you are free to act in accordance with your own will. This Rede is often interpreted as a call for personal responsibility and ethical behavior. The Wiccan Rede is often used as a guiding principle in decision-making and to promote positive actions and discourage negative ones.

The Wiccan Rede is not a commandment but rather a guideline for ethical behavior. It is up to the individual Wiccan to interpret the Rede and apply it to their lives. Some Wiccans interpret the Rede to mean they should avoid causing harm to any living being, while others take a more nuanced approach and understand that sometimes harm is necessary to protect themselves or others.

The Wiccan Rede is often viewed as a way to promote harmony and balance in the world. Wiccans believe their actions have a ripple effect affecting the world around them, and the Rede is a way to promote positive energy and discourage negative energy. By following the Rede, Wiccans can live in accordance with their beliefs and promote a more peaceful and harmonious world.

The Role of Magic in Wicca

Magic is an integral part of the Wiccan belief system. Wiccans believe that through ritual and intention, they can tap into the universe's power and manifest their desires, often done through spells designed to direct energy toward a specific goal. Wiccans also believe in karma, which states that the energy you put into the world will return to you. Therefore, magic is seen as a way to promote positive change in the world while taking responsibility for your actions.

Wiccan Traditions

Wicca is a highly diverse religion with many different Wiccan traditions existing today. Each tradition has its unique practices, beliefs, and rituals, and it can be difficult for outsiders to understand the differences. This section provides an overview of some of the most popular Wiccan traditions and explains the differences.

Gardnerian Wicca

One of the most well-known Wiccan traditions is Gardnerian Wicca, which Gerald Gardner founded in the 1950s. This tradition emphasizes the worship of the Horned God and the Mother Goddess and strongly emphasizes initiation and coven membership. Gardnerian Wicca is a highly structured tradition, and its members are expected to follow specific rules and practices.

- Gardnerian Wiccan rituals are typically held in a circle, representing the sacred space between the physical and the spiritual worlds. The circle is cast using various tools and symbols, like a wand or a sword, and the four elements (earth, air, fire, and water) are called upon to protect the space and those within it.
- The ritual is usually led by a High Priestess or High Priest, assisted by other coven members. The ritual can include elements such as chanting, drumming, dancing, and meditation. Coven members can take on specific roles during the ritual, like calling upon a particular element or deity.
- One of the key elements of Gardnerian Wiccan rituals is using the Great Rite. This rite involves a symbolic union of the Horned God and the Mother Goddess, representing the union of masculine and feminine energies. In some rituals, this involves a ritual blade (the athame) and a chalice of wine or other liquid.
- Another important aspect of Gardnerian Wiccan rituals is using magical energy to manifest desires or intentions. It involves spells, visualizations, or other techniques to focus and direct energy toward a particular goal.
- At the end of the ritual, the circle is opened, and the elements are thanked and released. Coven members usually share food and drink as a symbol of community and fellowship.

Alexandrian Wicca

Another popular Wiccan tradition is Alexandrian Wicca, founded by Alex Sanders in the 1960s. This tradition is similar to Gardnerian Wicca in many ways, but it places a greater emphasis on ceremonial magic and ritual. Alexandrian Wiccans often use various tools and symbols in their rituals, including swords, chalices, and wands.

- One of the key differences between Gardnerian and Alexandrian Wicca is the focus on using ceremonial magic in Alexandrian Wicca. While both traditions use ritual and magic to connect with the divine, Alexandrian Wiccans greatly emphasize using ceremonial magic techniques, such as ritual drama and specific correspondences and symbols.

- Alexandrian Wiccan rituals are similar in structure to Gardnerian rituals in terms of using a sacred circle, calling upon the elements and deities, and using the Great Rite. However, Alexandrian Wicca incorporates additional elements, such as ritual drama, trance work, and specific correspondences and symbols to focus and direct magical energy.
- Another key aspect of Alexandrian Wicca is the degree system, which consists of three degrees of initiation. As with Gardnerian Wicca, initiation into each degree involves specific teachings and practices, and initiates are expected to progress through the degrees to deepen their understanding and connection with the divine.
- Some other notable aspects of Alexandrian Wicca include the Rose Cross symbol, the emphasis on ceremonial magic, and the focus on the degree system as a means of spiritual growth and development.

Eclectic Wicca

Eclectic Wicca is a more modern tradition that emerged in the 1970s. This tradition is less structured than Gardnerian or Alexandrian Wicca and allows greater flexibility and individualism. Eclectic Wiccans often draw on various traditions and practices and create their rituals and practices based on their personal beliefs and experiences.

- Eclectic Wicca is a non-initiatory form of Wicca often practiced by individuals not drawn to any specific tradition or coven. It is a highly individualized Wicca allowing practitioners to pick and choose elements from various traditions and incorporate them into their practice.
- As the name suggests, eclectic Wicca blends different Wiccan traditions and other spiritual and religious practices. Practitioners of eclectic Wicca often create their own rituals, spells, and correspondences based on what resonates with them personally.
- Since eclectic Wicca is so personalized, the tradition has no initiation process or hierarchy. Many eclectic Wiccans practice alone, but some join groups or covens that are also eclectic in nature.

- One of the key aspects of eclectic Wicca is the emphasis on personal responsibility and the idea that the practitioner is the ultimate authority in their spiritual practice. So, there is no single "right" way to practice eclectic Wicca, and practitioners are encouraged to experiment and find what works best for them.
- Eclectic Wiccans draw inspiration from numerous sources, including different Wiccan traditions, other pagan and earth-based spiritualities, and even non-spiritual sources, like literature or pop culture. It makes eclectic Wicca a highly adaptable and flexible tradition that can be tailored to meet the needs and interests of individual practitioners.

There are many other Wiccan traditions, including Dianic Wicca, which places a greater emphasis on worshipping the goddess; Celtic Wicca, which draws on the traditions of ancient Celtic cultures; and Feri Wicca, which emphasizes ecstatic and trance-like experiences.

While each Wiccan tradition has its unique practices and beliefs, there are many similarities between them. Most Wiccans believe in worshiping a horned god and a mother goddess, and many strongly emphasize rituals and magic. However, the differences between traditions can be significant, and it is important for Wiccans to carefully consider their beliefs and values before choosing a particular tradition to follow.

Wiccan Festivals

Wiccan festivals, known as sabbats, are integral to the Wiccan belief system and calendar. Eight major sabbats are celebrated throughout the year, each marking an important point in the agricultural cycle and the changing seasons.

1. Samhain

Samhain is celebrated on October 31st and is considered the Wiccan New Year. It is a time to honor the ancestors, remember loved ones who have passed away, and let go of things no longer serving you. This festival is often associated with divination. It is believed the veil between the living and the dead is the thinnest on this day. People would leave food and drink offerings on their doorsteps to honor and welcome their ancestors or set a place at the table for them. This practice resembles the Day of the Dead celebrations in Mexico and other Latin American countries. As divination was a significant part of Samhain celebrations, many people believed that on this night, they could communicate with their ancestors' spirits and receive their messages and guidance. They would use divination tools like tarot cards, scrying mirrors, and Ogham staves to connect with the spirit world.

2. Yule

Yule is celebrated on the winter solstice, usually around December 21st. It marks the shortest day and longest night of the year. It is a time to celebrate the return of the Sun and the lengthening of the days. Yule is often associated with a god's birth and the Earth's renewal. Many modern pagans and Wiccans celebrate Yule as one of the eight sabbats, during which they gather in groups to perform rituals and cast spells or celebrate in a more solitary way. Whatever their approach, Yule is a time to honor the cycles of nature and celebrate the light that shines within everyone.

3. Imbolc

Imbolc is celebrated on February 1st or 2nd and marks the beginning of spring. It is a time to honor the goddess Brigid, who is associated with healing, creativity, and inspiration. Imbolc is often celebrated with purification rituals and lighting candles to represent the Sun's returning light. In addition to purification rituals and candle lighting, Imbolc is celebrated through feasting and exchanging gifts. Some traditional foods associated with the festival include dairy products, like milk and cheese, and bread and cakes.

4. Ostara

Ostara is celebrated on the spring equinox, usually around March 20th. It marks the balance between light and dark and the beginning of the planting season. Ostara is often associated with the goddess Eostre, who is associated with fertility, growth, and new beginnings. Ostara is a time to celebrate the power of the natural world and the interconnectedness of all things. Some common rituals practiced during Ostara include planting seeds, creating springtime crafts, and decorating eggs, symbolic of new life and rebirth.

5. Beltane

Beltane is celebrated on May 1st and marks the beginning of summer. It is a time to celebrate the union of the god and goddess and the Earth's fertility and abundance. Beltane is often celebrated with Maypole dances, flower crowns, and bonfires. Another key aspect of Beltane is lighting bonfires, which are seen as a way to purify and renew the land's energy. The fires are associated with the idea of transformation and crossing boundaries as people leap over the flames to symbolize their willingness to embrace change and growth.

6. Litha

Litha is celebrated on the summer solstice, usually around June 21st. It marks the longest day and shortest night of the year and a time to celebrate the Sun's power and the Earth's abundance. Litha is often associated with the god Lugh, who is associated with skills, craftsmanship, and creativity. At Litha, practitioners celebrate through numerous rituals and activities, including bonfires, feasts, and flower wreaths. Some people choose to spend time outdoors, soaking up the energy of the Sun and connecting with the natural world.

7. Lammas/Lughnasadh

Lammas or Lughnasadh is celebrated on August 1st and marks the beginning of the harvest season. It is a time to honor the god Lugh, associated with the grain harvest, and the goddess as the mother of the harvest. Lammas is often celebrated by baking bread and sharing a communal meal. Another key theme of Lammas is sacrifice. The harvest's first fruits are offered as a sacrifice to the gods in recognition of their providing for the people. This sacrifice is seen as a way to ensure continued abundance and prosperity in the coming year.

8. Mabon

Mabon is celebrated on the autumn equinox, usually around September 21st. It marks the balance between light and dark and the second harvest of the year. Mabon is often associated with the god Mabon, associated with rebirth and the turning of the seasons. The festivities include activities reflecting the abundance of the harvest, such as apple picking, wine-making, and creating harvest-themed crafts. Acts of charity and giving are common, recognizing that the blessings received are meant to be shared. As the Sun sets on Mabon, candles are lit, and people gather around the fire to share stories and reflect on the cycles of life and the passage of time.

Each festival is celebrated with specific rituals and practices designed to honor the specific energy and themes of the sabbat. These include offerings to the gods and goddesses, casting spells, lighting candles or fires, creating altars and sacred spaces, and sharing food and drink.

The importance of these festivals lies in their connection to the natural world and the changing of the seasons. By honoring the cycles of the Earth and the energy of each season, Wiccans believe they can cultivate a deeper connection to the natural world and the divine. These festivals serve as a time to come together as a community and celebrate shared beliefs.

Wiccan Structure and Roles

Wicca is a decentralized religion with no central authority or hierarchy. Its structure is based on covens, small groups of Wiccans who gather to practice their craft. Various roles and responsibilities are usually assigned to its members within a coven.

At the top of the Wiccan hierarchy is the High Priestess or High Priest, who is the leader of the coven. The High Priestess or High Priest is responsible for leading rituals, teaching new members, and guiding the spiritual development of the coven. They are responsible for maintaining the coven's traditions and ensuring that it adheres to Wiccan ethics and principles.

Below the High Priestess or High Priest are the coven members. Coven members are typically initiated into the coven and expected to participate in activities such as rituals and meetings. They can take on specific roles within the coven, like the coven's secretary or treasurer.

In addition to these roles, various degrees of initiation are within Wicca. These degrees signify a Wiccan's knowledge and experience level within the religion. First-degree Wiccans are typically new to the religion and have not yet been initiated into a coven. Second-degree Wiccans have been initiated into a coven and have a deeper understanding of Wiccan practices and beliefs. Third-degree Wiccans are considered High Priests or High Priestesses and have the knowledge and experience necessary to lead their covens.

Simple Full Moon Ritual

The objective of this ritual is to honor the full Moon and connect with its energy. Through this ritual, you have the opportunity to deepen your understanding and appreciation of the natural cycles and rhythms of the Earth and the Moon and align yourself with the powerful energies during the full Moon phase.

Materials:
- A candle (preferably white or silver)
- Matches or a lighter

- A piece of paper and a pen
- A small dish with water
- Any additional ritual tools (optional)

Instructions:
1. Choose a quiet, outdoor space where you can see the full Moon. Alternatively, you can set up an altar indoors with a representation of the Moon, like a picture or a statue.
2. Begin by grounding and centering yourself. Take a few deep breaths and visualize yourself becoming fully present in the moment.
3. Light the candle and hold it up to the Moon. Say a simple blessing, such as "Blessed be the light of the full Moon."
4. Write down whatever you want to release or let go of on the piece of paper and the intentions or goals you want to manifest in the upcoming month. Fold the paper and place it on the dish of water.
5. Hold your hands over the dish and say, *"I release what no longer serves me and open myself to new opportunities and growth."* Visualize the water absorbing the negative energy or unwanted thoughts and feelings.
6. Take a moment to feel the full Moon's energy and connect with your intuition and inner wisdom.
7. When you are ready, blow out the candle and say, *"So, mote it be,"* meaning *"Let it be so."*
8. Dispose of the paper and water in a way that is safe and respectful to the environment.
9. Close the ritual by thanking the deities or spirits you called upon and thanking yourself for taking the time to honor the full Moon.

Despite being thousands of years old, Wicca and neopaganism remain relevant spiritual practices for many individuals in modern times. As society becomes more disconnected from nature and traditional spirituality, many people are turning to Wicca and neopaganism as a way to reconnect with the natural world and their spirituality. Wicca and neopaganism allow individuals to create their own spiritual practices based on their beliefs and values. This way, Wicca and neopaganism remain important and relevant practices for many individuals in the modern world.

Chapter 8: Applying Your Pagan Beliefs to Daily Life

This final chapter takes a practical approach to what it means to be a modern pagan and how to go about it in your everyday life. This chapter will provide instructions on how to find a deity to work with, set up an altar, celebrate pagan holidays, start a journal or grimoire, connect with other pagans, and more.

Finding Your Patron or Matron Deity

While having a patron or matron deity is optional, they can help you find your path by guiding you in the right direction. They can protect and empower you during your pagan work (magical or otherwise) and help you heal if needed. However, if you decide to find a patron or matron deity, you should start by exploring yourself. Remember, the power comes from within you. Any energy you receive from a divine being or nature will only amplify the power you already have. So, the best way to find the deity to empower you is to look for those whose correspondents resonate with you.

Reading about deities you find interesting may help you connect with them.*

Research the deities you find interesting. While reading about each particular god or goddess, listen to your intuition. If you feel particularly drawn to one, dive deeper into their backgrounds, history, myths, and correspondences. Learn how other modern-day practitioners work with the god or goddess. If you're absolutely certain about wanting to work with a particular deity, contact them by dedicating a prayer to them. Alternatively, you can light a candle and gaze into its flames while chanting the deity's name. However, sometimes simply showing interest in them will earn their attention, and they will contact you.

If the deity you have chosen doesn't communicate with you right away, don't worry. They might feel you don't need their help at that moment. Or, it could be that you don't know how to recognize or decipher their signs yet. While you can express how you would like to be contacted, some deities have their own ways. For example, if you've addressed them in prayer before sleeping, they might approach you in your dreams.

Consider holding an introductory ritual if you struggle to connect with your chosen matron or patron deity. Here is how to do it:

1. Dedicate a small altar to them, and adorn it with their correspondences and symbols.
2. Light a candle in their name, call on them, and introduce yourself.
3. State your name and your intention of forming a relationship with them.

4. Express your gratitude for any blessing you might receive in the future.
5. Repeat if needed in a few days.

When you start working with your matron or patron, feel free to set boundaries for your relationship. As with any relationship, working with a pagan deity is a two-way street. You should count on their blessing just as much as they should count on you honoring and celebrating them. They should listen to you just as much as you should listen to them. If the deity you made contact with turns out to be a bad match for you, feel free to end your relationship. Remember, you don't have to settle for the first deity you feel drawn to, nor must you keep working with the same matron or patron deity all your life. So many options are available, and you might need different assistance at the various stages of your life.

Setting Up Your Altar

While having an altar isn't mandatory in pagan practice, it can help you channel your energy into your intention. It helps link with a deity, spirit, and your spirituality. Here is how to set up a simple pagan altar.

Choose the Placement

Many pagans practice outdoors, but if you prefer to do it indoors, feel free to place your altar inside your home. Either way, it should be where you can work without distractions and where it won't bother you or anyone else living in your home. Most practitioners who use indoor altars opt for placing them in their bedrooms as this is the most secluded room in a house.

You can use an old table or dresser as the base of your altar, you'll cover it anyway, so it won't matter how it looks. Or, if you have limited space, you can always set it up on your dresser, bookcase, or windowsill. A naturally flat surface, like a large tree trunk, will work if you're setting up an outside altar.

Consider the Direction

The direction you set up your altar facing depends on your practice, preferences, and available space. Suppose you're working with limited space or aren't sure which direction would fit your purpose, create an east-facing altar. In that case, this is the direction of the rising sun, which is powerful in many pagan practices.

Decide on the Style
The style of your altar depends on the pagan path you follow. If you wish to dedicate it to a specific entity or holiday, the style will be influenced by their associations. Or, if you haven't decided on a particular spiritual path or purpose for your altar, go with your gut feelings. Let your intuition decide on the style; it might reveal the course you should follow.

Choose the Adornments
Use their association and representatives if working with a particular deity (or planning to work with one). If you have a matron or patron deity, place their symbols on the center of your altar. If you're working with your ancestors, use their representation or their personal items if you have any. If you want to empower yourself, include your personal items.

Other suggested items to place on the altar:

- Divination tools
- Symbols of protection
- Crystals
- Wands and athames
- Grimoire or book of shadows
- Candles
- The representation of the four elements
- Loose herbs
- Talismans or amulets

Celebrating Esbats and Sabbats

Pagans worldwide celebrate esbats (Moon rituals) and Sabbats (seasonal festivities) in a myriad of ways. Some traditions are community-based, while others are highly personal. As a beginner, you should focus on establishing personal traditions for these holidays. It will help you understand their significance and inspire you to dedicate more time to them. Here are suggested practices to celebrate pagan holidays.

Decorating
Nearly all pagan rituals and ceremonies performed at esbats and sabbats use candles. Decorating candles is a great way to celebrate any pagan holiday. Use colors, herbs, and other materials associated with the holiday. You can let your creativity loose and make as many candles as

you wish. You'll use candles for your altar, as adornments for your home, or as gifts.

You can make decorations with flowers and other elements of nature. Whichever material you use should be associated with the specific holiday. For example, some herbs have protective abilities, and making a wreath from them for your front door can be an excellent complementary practice for protection spells and rituals.

Preparing Tools

Some pagans prefer to prepare their own oils, herbal blends, symbols, representations, and other tools in their practice. While you can purchase your tools pre-made, making them can be satisfying and spiritually uplifting, especially if you're preparing for a sacred day or holiday. You'll have a more powerful connection with your tools, as they'll be automatically charged with your energy.

Cleansing

Whichever esbat or sabbat you're preparing for, it doesn't hurt to cleanse yourself and your property from negative influences. Each holiday marks a momentous event on a pagan calendar and represents the beginning of a new period. It's always better to start a new period with a clean slate or, better yet, be empowered with positive energy. Here are suggestions on how to cleanse yourself and your home:

- Smudging
- Incense
- Cleansing bath
- Sprinkling salt
- Basking in moonlight
- Using a cleansing spell
- Asking a deity to help you cleanse
- Using a cleaning talisman or pouch made of herbs
- Drinking herbal tea
- Walking in nature
- Standing in sunlight
- Surrounding yourself with houseplants

Preparing Meals

Whether you celebrate an esbat or sabbat with a large community, your friends, your family, or alone, preparing meals associated with that holiday is a fantastic way to get into the spirit. Look into what other modern practitioners of your chosen pagan path recommend preparing for a particular holiday, and pick your favorite recipes. Even if you live with other non-pagan family members, you can still ask them to help you prepare the meals. It can be a terrific activity for families with children as they usually like learning and doing something new.

Creating a Logbook, Journal, or Grimoire

Recording your practice is a great way to monitor the progress of your spiritual journey. If you're just starting, create a logbook of rituals and acts you've performed throughout the day, week, or month. It will help you keep track of the planned tasks and ensure you don't forget to implement them regularly. The more pagan practices you incorporate into your schedule, the closer you discover your spiritual path.

Start a journal if you practice divination, attempt to communicate with your spiritual guides, or want a more detailed characterization of your practices. Unlike a logbook (which only has data about specific tasks), a journal can contain the signs and messages you've received, your emotions regarding specific tools, or anything else you might want to document along your journey.

If you also practice witchcraft, you can start a grimoire. A grimoire is a book that keeps track of magical practices. It can contain correspondence of deities and ancestors, sabbats, esbats, and other sacred days you celebrate. Or your preferred ways to cast spells, specific spells and rituals you've done, divination methods, astrological correspondences, herbs and recipes for healing agents, and crystals. It can include topics you feel inspired by or want to learn.

Whether you create a logbook, journal, or grimoire, remember to keep it safe. You have a personal connection to it, and any energy the book picks up can affect you. Cleanse it often and consecrate it if necessary.

Connecting with Other Pagans

Connecting to other pagan groups and communities is a great way to gain more knowledge and understanding of a particular spiritual path. In these modern times, there are plenty of ways to find like-minded people near you or even on the other side of the world. If you don't mind the distance or just looking for advice, look for pagan groups on social media sites and forums. Whichever pagan path you wish to follow, you'll find the group that suits your needs.

If you prefer to find people you can meet, exchange experiences with, and celebrate sabbats, esbats, and other pagan holidays, or worship deities together, look around in your area. Start with occult bookshops, as these typically have posted notices of other pagans looking for communities or pagan communities looking to gather new members.

Whichever way you get in touch with other pagans, feel free to share your spiritual journey with them, no matter how short. Maybe your experience will help someone struggling to find their path or has veered off an already established path and looking for their way back.

Pagan Life To-Dos

Part of embarking on a pagan path is to cater to your spiritual needs. Fortunately, many ways exist to incorporate simple daily pagan rituals without affecting your schedule. Following a to-do list will help you, and you don't have to check every item on the list every day. Feel free to pick and choose a few that can fit into your routine. The overall goal is to create a habit of daily pagan rituals to help you get closer to the pagan lifestyle.

Here is the checklist of pagan rituals:

- Light a candle. You can say a quick prayer of gratitude to your matron or patron deity, ancestors, or other spiritual guides with whom you have been working.

- Make offerings to a deity. You can keep this ritual as simple as you want. For example, you can offer them a cup of coffee or water or share a meal with them.

- Make offerings to your ancestors. Remember to offer their favorite items.

- Rise to greet the Sun. The Sun is fundamental in most pagan traditions. Spending a couple of minutes basking in sunlight after you wake up can help you take advantage of its energy.

- Do yoga. Even one or two positions daily will do wonders for your spiritual life.

- Go for a walk (preferably in nature) to reconnect with nature's power. During lunch hour, 10 minutes will do the trick.

However, you should aim for regular walks outside.

- Try dream journaling. Set a journal at your bedside, so you can record your dreams as soon as you wake up. It can help you connect and communicate with spirits, deities, and your intuition.
- Mediate. Daily meditation is recommended for most spiritual seekers. Whether you listen to a guided meditation or let your intuition lead you, it doesn't matter.
- Pay attention to nature. Be more vigilant of your surroundings to notice the little signs and omens nature sends you.
- Light incense. Similarly to candlelight, the incense's scent is soothing and grounding. It creates the perfect atmosphere for mediation, rituals, and magical work.
- Read a spiritual book. Even if you have only 15 minutes to set aside for reading, use it to learn more about the spiritual path you've chosen to follow.
- Spend time with your pets. If you have pets, spending time with them would be the perfect pagan way to honor nature.
- Light a red candle in the kitchen. This ritual honors your ancestors and symbolizes the hearth (fireplace), which most modern homes don't have. However, it was indispensable in pagan traditions.
- Cleanse yourself and your area with smoke. Some pagans call it a smudging ritual. It involves lighting a bundle of dried herbs and enveloping yourself and the space or object you want to cleanse from bad energies in their smoke.
- Spend time with your family. This is another essential pagan ritual recommended daily. Even if you have 10-15 minutes to show how much you care, do it.
- Write a book of shadows or grimoire. This book can help you monitor your progress on your spiritual journey and learn to follow the pagan path you find fulfilling.
- Wear a crystal. You can wear jewelry with crystal in the morning or put the stone in your pocket or bag. Either way, if you have charged it with positive energy, it will protect you and enhance your power throughout the day.

- Start and tend to a garden. Whether you have a place for a few pots on your windowsill or a full-size garden in your backyard, tending to your garden is a very satisfying pagan ritual.
- Exercise. With the modern, sedentary lifestyle, exercising can be a pagan ritual. It can help you remember all your ancestors' physical work to sustain their families. Without their efforts, you wouldn't be where you are.
- Drink herbal tea. Brewing herbal tea in the morning and sipping it is a great way to slow down and prepare for your upcoming spiritual challenges.
- Read a card or rune. If you practice divination (or want to enhance your spirituality), pick a card or rune every morning and contemplate its meaning.
- Use herbs for cooking. Herbs have incredible healing properties, and your ancestors knew this. They used them in their daily lives, and so can you.
- Freshen up your altar or shrine. Check your sacred place daily for ashes, dust, and debris, and clean it if necessary. Replace your offerings (especially if you have food items) or exchange them for different ones.
- Gaze at the Moon. Just as sitting in the sunlight can help you recharge your energies, so can gazing at the Moon. You can go outside when the sky is clear or sit at an open window.
- Plan the next sabbat or esbat. If a pagan holiday is nearing, making small steps toward it could be a great daily ritual. Research what you need to do during that holiday and plan for it.
- Call a pagan friend. Whether you need advice on moving forward with your spiritual journey or need a little boost of confidence, talking to a like-minded person can help you immensely.
- Ground and center yourself. You don't have to do meditation or other mindfulness techniques to ground yourself. It takes simple actions like quieting your mind, walking barefoot, or touching a tree to take advantage of nature's centering power.
- Learn more about your patron or matron deity. Taking even a few minutes daily to learn about the god or goddess you want to

connect with will help you honor them and enrich your relationship.

Appendix: A-Z of the Wheel of the Year

As the seasons turn and the cycles of nature unfold, humans have long celebrated the turning points of the year. From ancient times, pagan and polytheistic cultures throughout Europe marked the solstices, equinoxes, and other significant moments with festivals, feasts, and rituals. These celebrations honor nature's gods and goddesses, acknowledge the seasons' changes, and offer a time for reflection, renewal, and community. While some traditions have been lost over time, many continue to be practiced and adapted by modern pagans and polytheists. This chapter explores a selection of these festivals from across Europe, from the well-known to the more obscure, and discovers the rich tapestry of customs and beliefs making the Wheel of the Year.

1. Alban Arthan (AL-ban AHR-than) - December 20th or 21st

Alban Arthan, known as the winter solstice, is a festival celebrating the Sun's rebirth and the return of light after the darkest day of the year. It is a time when the natural world lies dormant, and people gather to kindle the flame of hope and renewal. Many pagan and polytheistic traditions honor the god or goddess of the Sun, such as the Welsh Mabon, the Irish Lugh, and the Roman Sol Invictus. Alban Arthan is a time for introspection, for letting go of the old and welcoming the new. It is a time to celebrate the joys of family and community, share stories, feasts, and gifts, and honor the spirits of the land and the ancestors who came before us. Some popular customs include lighting candles, decorating trees, and holding bonfires. For many, Alban Arthan is a profound and meaningful festival reminding them of the beauty and resilience of the human spirit in the face of darkness.

2. Alban Eilir (AL-ban EYE-leer) - March 20th or 21st

The festival of Alban Eilir, pronounced AL-ban EYE-leer, is celebrated on either March 20th or 21st, marking the arrival of the spring equinox. This ancient pagan festival celebrates the emergence of the natural world from the depths of winter as the earth awakens and new life flourishes. It is a time of balance, when the day and night are equal, and the promise of longer, warmer days are just around the corner. Alban Eilir is honored by many polytheistic traditions, with many cultures offering their own interpretation of the festival. From the Celtic goddess Brigid to the Germanic goddess Ostara and the Greek goddess Persephone, Alban Eilir represents the triumph of fertility and growth over the darkness and cold of winter. The festival is a time to set intentions, plant new seeds, and embrace the renewal of the natural world. It is a time to reconnect with nature, breathe in the fresh air, and revel in the beauty of the world around you. During this festival, people decorate eggs, clean their homes, and engage in other symbolic acts to commemorate the occasion.

3. Brigid (BREE-jid) - February 1st or 2nd

Brigid is a Celtic goddess representing inspiration, creativity, and healing. Her festival is celebrated on February 1st or 2nd, marking the beginning of spring in the Celtic calendar. Brigid is associated with the sacred flame, and her festival is often marked by lighting candles and bonfires. The festival is known as Imbolc, meaning "in the belly" in Old Irish. It represents the time of year when the first stirrings of new life can be felt beneath the earth's surface. In Ireland, Brigid is revered as a patron saint, and her festival is celebrated as St. Brigid's Day, with traditions like making Brigid's crosses and leaving out offerings of milk and bread for her. Across Europe, Brigid's festival is a time for purification and renewal and honoring the divine feminine and the power of nature.

4. Cerealia - April 12th-19th

The Cerealia was an ancient Roman festival celebrated in honor of the goddess Ceres, the goddess of agriculture and grain. The festival was held annually from April 12th to April 19th and was one of the most important celebrations of the Roman calendar. During the Cerealia, the Romans would honor Ceres by offering milk and honey as well as having processions and conducting various rituals. In ancient times, the Cerealia was a time for farmers to celebrate the arrival of spring and the beginning of the agricultural season. It was a time to give thanks to Ceres for the bounty of the land and ask for her continued blessings throughout the growing season. The festival allowed people to come together and socialize, enjoy the warm weather, and indulge in food, drink, and entertainment. Today, the Cerealia is no longer celebrated as it once was in ancient Rome. However, the legacy of Ceres lives on in the modern world through many traditions and customs associated with agriculture and the celebration of spring. From planting seeds in the garden to enjoying a delicious meal made with fresh, locally grown produce, the spirit of Ceres can be felt in how people honor the earth and the bounty it provides.

5. Feast of Aphrodite - July 23rd

The Feast of Aphrodite falls on July 23rd, celebrating the Greek goddess of love, beauty, and fertility. This festival is associated with the height of summer and the full bloom of nature, making it an ideal time to honor Aphrodite and seek her blessings for love, fertility, and creative inspiration. In ancient Greece, the Feast of Aphrodite was celebrated with offerings of flowers, honey, incense, music, dancing, and feasting. It was a time for lovers to express their devotion to one another and for unmarried women to seek Aphrodite's guidance in finding a suitable partner. Today, modern practitioners of Hellenic Paganism and other traditions honoring the Greek gods and goddesses continue to celebrate the Feast of Aphrodite. This festival is a time for rituals of love and fertility and artistic and creative endeavors. Celebrations include offerings of flowers and honey, dancing, and reading poetry or love spells.

6. Feast of Hekate - November 16th

On November 16th, pagan communities worldwide celebrate the Feast of Hekate, a festival dedicated to the Greek goddess of magic, witchcraft, and the crossroads. Traditionally, this festival was observed with offerings of food, incense, and other gifts at crossroads and other liminal spaces, where Hekate was believed to be most present. It was a time for performing magic and divination and seeking Hekate's guidance in matters of life and death. Modern practitioners of Hellenic Paganism and other traditions honoring Hekate continue to celebrate the Feast of Hekate. The celebrations include lighting candles, casting spells, and offering food, incense, and other gifts. This festival is a time for reconnecting with the divine and seeking magical blessings for the year ahead. The Feast of Hekate holds special significance for those honoring the goddess of magic and witchcraft. The liminal spaces associated with Hekate represent the crossroads between the physical and spiritual worlds, and the festival offers an opportunity to explore this concept further through ritual and magic.

7. Harvest Home - September 21st or 22nd

As the days grow shorter and the nights longer, the Harvest Home festival marks the end of summer and the beginning of autumn. Celebrated on September 21st or 22nd, it is a time of gratitude for the bountiful harvest that sustains through the long winter months. The Harvest Home festival was a time of feasting and revelry in ancient times, as communities came together to share the fruits of their labor. It was a time for singing, dancing, and telling stories around the fire as the earth turned inward and the leaves began to fall. Today, the Harvest Home festival is celebrated in many parts of Europe, with traditional customs, like crowning a Harvest Queen, decorating the village with boughs of wheat and corn, and blessing the crops. It is a time to give thanks for the earth's abundance and to honor the hard work of farmers and growers who provide food throughout the year.

8. Krampusnacht (KRAHM-pus-nahkt) - December 5th

Krampusnacht, celebrated on December 5th, is a festival with a darker edge. While many associate the winter holiday season with warmth, love, and light, Krampusnacht is a time when fear and mischief take center stage. Originating in Alpine regions of Europe, Krampusnacht is named after Krampus, a horned, demonic creature said to punish naughty children while his benevolent counterpart, St. Nicholas, rewards the good. In many towns and villages, revelers dress up as Krampus and parade through the streets, terrifying young and old with their gruesome costumes and playful pranks. Despite its macabre tone, Krampusnacht is a beloved tradition in many parts of Europe. It is a way to balance light and dark and good and evil. It is a reminder that there is always a balance to be struck in life.

9. Lupercalia (loo-per-KAY-lee-ah) - February 13th-15th

Lupercalia, a festive celebration tracing its roots to ancient Rome, is a time to honor the god of fertility and protect the city from evil spirits. The festival, held from February 13th to 15th, was dedicated to the god Lupercus and was essential to the city's cultural identity. The priests would wear animal skins, and women were whipped with strips of hide to ensure their fertility and protect them from evil. The festival's association with the founding of Rome adds to its historical significance. The sacrifice of goats and dogs made it a somber event. While Lupercalia is no longer celebrated in its original form, it remains a meaningful time for modern pagans and Wiccans. They have adapted the festival to celebrate the coming of spring and to honor the god of fertility. Nowadays, Lupercalia is a time of feasting, during which participants share food and drink and partake in rituals to welcome the change of season. The spirit of Lupercalia lives on in the modern world as a time when people connect with nature and each other. It is a time to celebrate life and recognize the importance of fertility and growth.

10. Midsummer - June 21st

Midsummer, known as Litha or the Summer Solstice, is a time when the Sun is at its highest point in the sky and the day is the longest. It's celebrated in various ways throughout Europe, with bonfires a common element in many cultures. For example, in Sweden, Midsummer is one of the biggest holidays, and people gather around a maypole to sing and dance traditional folk songs. In other parts of Europe, herbs and flowers are gathered for various magical rituals. It's a time for celebrating the earth's abundance and giving thanks for the harvest to come. The Midsummer celebration is a reminder of the natural world's power and beauty and the importance of living harmoniously with it.

11. Panathenaia (pan-ath-uh-NAY-uh) - July 28th

The Panathenaia, celebrated on July 28th, is a festival dedicated to the Greek goddess Athena, the patron goddess of Athens. It was one of ancient Athens's most important religious festivals and was celebrated every four years. The festival began with a procession through the city, culminating in a grand sacrifice of 100 oxen to the goddess. The festival included athletic and musical competitions and dramatic performances in the Theatre of Dionysus. Panathenaia was a time for Athenians to come together and celebrate their culture and heritage, and it remains a significant cultural event in modern Greece. In modern times, the Panathenaia is still celebrated in Athens and other parts of Greece. The festival retains many traditional elements, such as the procession and the athletic and musical competitions. However, modern celebrations include more contemporary events, such as fireworks displays, concerts, and cultural exhibitions. The festival is an important time for Greeks to celebrate their cultural heritage and unite in a spirit of unity and national pride.

12. Perchtenlauf (PERK-ten-louf) - January 5th or 6th

Perchtenlauf, known as the "Night of the Witches," is a winter festival celebrated in Austria and other parts of Europe on January 5th or 6th. The festival is believed to have its roots in pagan traditions and is dedicated to the goddess Perchta, who roamed the Earth during the winter months. During the festival, men dress in elaborate costumes and masks, representing the Perchten, or "wild spirits." They roam the streets, making noise with bells and wooden sticks to drive away evil spirits and welcome the new year. The festival includes bonfires, feasting, and traditional dance performances. The Perchtenlauf is a time for communities to come together, celebrate their traditions, and banish the darkness of winter with the light of hope and renewal. Today, the festival remains a cherished part of Austrian and European culture, with many communities preserving its ancient customs and adding their unique touches to the celebration.

13. Veneralia (ven-ur-AY-lee-uh) - April 1st

On April 1st, the ancient Romans celebrated Veneralia, a festival dedicated to Venus, the goddess of love and beauty. Veneralia was a time for people to honor and appease the goddess, hoping for her blessings and protection in love and fertility. The festival was marked by offering flowers and incense at Venus' temples and shrines and the ritual washing of her statues. In some parts of Rome, young girls would gather at Venus' temple to ask for her favor in finding a husband, while married women would pray for the health and prosperity of their marriages. Veneralia was a time of great joy and celebration, marked by feasting, drinking, and music. Today, the festival is largely forgotten, but its influence can still be seen in the modern celebration of April Fool's Day, which falls on the same date.

14. Walpurgis Night (WAL-pur-gis nahyt) - April 30th

On the eve of May Day, witches and revelers gather to celebrate Walpurgis Night, a festival with deep roots in pagan tradition. Named after Saint Walpurga, an eighth-century abbess renowned for her healing powers, the festival marks the arrival of spring and the awakening of nature's fertility. In many parts of Europe, people light bonfires, dance around Maypoles, and engage in other traditional rituals to welcome the season of growth and renewal. But Walpurgis Night also has a darker side, as it is said to be a time when the veil between the living and the dead is the thinnest. According to legend, witches and other supernatural beings come out and wreak havoc on unsuspecting villagers. Despite this, the festival remains a time for joy and merriment, as people gather with friends and family to celebrate the arrival of spring and honor their ancestors' traditions.

The world is full of fascinating and diverse pagan and polytheistic festivals celebrated for centuries. From the joyful harvest celebrations to the solemn rites of honoring the dead, these festivals offer a glimpse into ancient cultures' rich and complex beliefs. While many of these traditions have faded over time, some continue to be celebrated in modern times, connecting to the collective past and celebrating cultural heritage. These festivals are a reminder of the power of community, the importance of tradition, and the enduring human need to connect with something greater than self.

Conclusion

As this book has shown, Paganism is an umbrella term for several closely related religions. European Paganism practitioners share the same core beliefs, from the reverence of nature to the universal acceptance of polytheism. They view life as a cycle, similar to nature, which changes with the seasons. It is born, dies, and is revived as a human soul can be reincarnated or live on in the spiritual world. The latter refers to ancestral spirits, significant in Paganism as deities. Ancestors and spirit guides can be summoned for guidance, healing, and protection. The pagan gods and goddesses are typically associated with one aspect of life, although many pagans have deities who embody different aspects and more than one face or name. Several parts of pagan practices are linked to heavenly bodies, with the Sun and the Moon referenced in many myths, legends, and traditions.

This book has explored how the key points of the pagan belief system were incorporated into the various forms of European Paganism, including Celtic Paganism and Druidry, Asatru and Norse Paganism, Germanic Paganism, Slavic Paganism, Greek Polytheism, and Wicca. Naturally, since some of these religions are older than others, there are often wide variations of traditions, even customs related to the same practices or entities. The gods and goddesses have different names and associations and might even be honored through different rituals and ceremonies. However, since the older religions have only survived through oral traditions, their diversified evolution is only comparable to the development of the newer ones to some extent.

Hopefully, the relevant chapters have given you sufficient insight to pique your interest and decide which pagan path to follow. If yes, the last chapter should help you incorporate your chosen path into your life. If you have yet to determine your course, incorporating elements of Paganism into your schedule will help you to get in touch with your spirituality. Remember, Paganism is a highly spiritual and personal practice. While it is beneficial for pagans to share their ideas and rely on like-minded people, you can't forget that your power lies within you. Even little pagan rituals like walking in nature, meditating for 10 minutes, or reciting a prayer to a deity to which you feel drawn can help you find your path and purpose. If you wish to delve deeper into a specific practice and celebrate pagan holidays, refer to this book's Witches Wheel of the Year. It will help you find those that fit your path, needs, and preferences.

Part 2: Norse Paganism

Unlocking the Secrets of Norse Magic, Elder Futhark Runes, Spells, Asatru, Shamanic Rituals, and Divination

Introduction

Norse Paganism, or *Heathenism*, is a complex and fascinating belief system that has captured worldwide attention. At its core, Norse Paganism is a spiritual tradition honoring the gods and goddesses of the ancient Norse pantheon, as well as the spirits of nature, ancestors, and other supernatural entities. While Norse Paganism has been practiced for thousands of years, it has experienced a resurgence in recent times, thanks in part to the growing popularity of neo-paganism and Wicca. Many modern practitioners, sometimes called *Norse Wiccans*, draw on ancient Norse beliefs and practices to create a vibrant and dynamic form of spirituality that is uniquely their own.

One of the most distinctive aspects of Norse Paganism is its emphasis on the interconnectedness of all things. According to this worldview, everything in the universe is connected, and all things are imbued with a divine spark. This belief is reflected in the many myths and legends of the Norse pantheon, which depicts the gods and goddesses as intimately involved in the natural world, shaping and influencing the forces of nature through their actions and deeds. Another essential feature of Norse Paganism is its emphasis on community and kinship. Many modern practitioners of Norse Paganism, inspired by the ancient Viking tradition of the Thing, or public assembly, gather to celebrate festivals, share stories, and honor the gods and goddesses in a communal setting. This sense of community and shared purpose is a powerful source of strength and inspiration for many modern practitioners of Norse Paganism, helping them connect with the natural world and each other deeply and meaningfully.

One of the most intriguing aspects of Norse Paganism is its connection to the natural world. In ancient times, the Norse people lived in a harsh and unforgiving land where the forces of nature were ever-present and often dangerous. To survive, they developed a deep reverence for the natural world, seeing it as both powerful and sacred. This reverence for nature is reflected in many aspects of Norse Paganism, from worshiping nature spirits and deities associated with the elements to using natural materials in rituals and ceremonies. Modern practitioners of Norse Paganism have carried on this tradition, finding inspiration and guidance in the rhythms of the natural world.

Throughout this book, you'll explore the rich and diverse world of Norse Paganism, delving into its history, mythology, and practices. You'll learn how this ancient spiritual tradition has evolved and adapted and continues to inspire and inform modern neo-paganism, Wicca, and other related belief systems. Whether you are a seasoned practitioner of Norse Paganism or simply curious about this fascinating spiritual tradition, this book offers a unique and insightful look into one of human history's most enduring and powerful belief systems.

Chapter 1: Paganism 101

This chapter will introduce you to the pagan religion and the terms "Paganism" and "pagan." Besides receiving an in-depth analysis of Paganism's ancient and modern historical background, you'll also learn about the various pagan religions that exist and have existed throughout the world. Lastly, you will
l explore Paganism's principle beliefs and traditional practices.

What Is Paganism?

Paganism is one of the oldest spiritual traditions in the world. It predates Christianity, although the term "pagan" is believed to have been coined by Christian practitioners who used it to label everyone who didn't share their belief system. The word "pagan" comes from the Latin word "paganus," which means "country dweller" or "of the earth." Over time, the term has been reclaimed by many pagans and is now used proudly to describe themselves.

Pagans worship nature and its creatures.⁹

Paganism is an umbrella term used to describe various earth-based spiritual traditions. It generally refers to an earth-based religion where practitioners worship and respect nature and its creatures. Pagans believe that universal energy can be found in all things natural and often look to nature for guidance and inspiration.

Over the centuries, Paganism has evolved and changed to reflect the cultures and beliefs of its practitioners. Today, there are many different forms of Paganism practiced all over the world. Because of this, it is one of the most diverse religious movements in the world. It's not a centralized belief system like other widespread religions, either. Practitioners neither follow a strict doctrine nor gather regularly in places of worship.

Origin of Paganism

Paganism is thought to have originated in pre-Christian Europe, possibly developing out of a need to explain common occurrences in the natural world and people's place within it. Historians believe pagan ideas were likely developed in small, tight-knit communities where everyone knew and trusted one another. As these communities grew, the beliefs became more organized until they became religions.

Pagan beliefs likely first developed in Europe and Asia, and some can be traced back to many ancient cultures, including the Celts, Greeks, and Romans. However, Paganism can be found in almost every culture across the globe. It was widely practiced all over Europe, but with the rise of Christianity in the 4th century, it started declining. However, it was still practiced until the 10th century to some extent. In the 1500s, the Renaissance was a period of intense interest in classical culture. During this time, Paganism was incorporated into the arts, music, literature, and many other aspects of life.

Paganism began to re-emerge as a distinct religious movement in the 20th century. In the United Kingdom, the Pagan Federation was founded in 1971 to support Pagans of all traditions. Since then, the trend has grown steadily throughout the world.

Many of the world's major religions, including Christianity, Islam, and Judaism, have roots in Paganism. During the Middle Ages, when the Christianization of the European continent was in full swing, Christianity began to replace many of the older pagan traditions. However, people continued to practice in secrecy, often disguising their practice as Christian traditions. Those who didn't and those who were discovered were persecuted and executed by the Church. Despite centuries of persecution, Paganism has survived and is now thriving again in many parts of the world. Today, there are an estimated two million pagans worldwide, and Paganism has become one of the fastest-growing religions in the world.

History of Paganism

Paganism in Europe

Since ancient times, Paganism in Europe has been associated with nature worship, magic, and deep reverence for the natural world. Back then, the land was mostly forest, and people lived in small villages or were tribes tending to their farms or herds. There were many different tribes, each one with unique customs and beliefs.

England has a rich history of Paganism, dating back to the Bronze Age. The pagan tribes of England worshipped various gods and goddesses, including the god of the sun, the god of the moon, and the goddess of fertility. The most well-known pagan deity in England is the goddess Brigid, the Lady of the Lake. She is associated with fire, healing, and poetry. Another popular deity is the Horned God, associated with hunting and animals. Paganism was the dominant religion in England until the arrival of Christianity in the 7th century. Soon after, it started to decline as the Christian church became more powerful. By the 13th century, it had all but disappeared from England. However, it experienced a resurgence in the 18th and 19th centuries when people began to explore other religions.

Like England, Ireland was also a pagan country before the arrival of Christianity in the 5th century. However, pagans there practice a variety of ancient traditions. These traditions include the construction of temporary altars or shrines, the lighting of fires, and the offering of gifts to the gods and goddesses. They also celebrate various seasonal festivals, such as Beltane and Mabon. Neo-Paganism in Ireland is a modern movement that revives ancient pagan traditions. It is practiced by a small minority, most of whom are members of the Pagan Federation of Ireland.

Paganism was also the dominant religion in Iceland before its Christianization in 1000 AD. It is thought that Paganism first arrived in Iceland around 900 AD, brought by settlers from Scandinavia and the British Isles. Paganism continued to be practiced in Iceland even after Christianity became the dominant religion. Paganism declined in popularity after that, but some Icelanders still practiced it into the 13th century. After that, Christianity became the only religion practiced in Iceland. The Icelandic Pagans also believed in many other beings, such as elves, dwarves, giants, and trolls. Some of these beings were thought to be helpful, while others were considered to be dangerous. Pagan beliefs and practices were passed down orally from generation to generation.

Norway and Sweden are the two countries with the most colorful and long-lasting pagan traditions. Even though Norway converted to Christianity around the late 10th or early 11th centuries, the country was slow to give up its pagan ways. Swedish pagans, on the other hand, didn't accept Christianity until the middle or late 11th century, allowing Paganism to flourish well after the 12th century.

Paganism in America

American paganism has a long and complicated history. It is difficult to say precisely when or how Paganism first arrived on the shores of the United States. Some believe that the ancient indigenous peoples of North and South America practiced it in a specific form, while others believe that the first pagans in America were European immigrants who brought their own beliefs and practices with them.

European colonists brought various pagan traditions, including Druidry, Celtic Shamanism, Norse Magic, and Wicca, to the Americas. These traditions mixed and mingled with each other and the native beliefs already present in America, creating a rich and diverse pagan tradition.

Paganism continued to grow in popularity throughout the 19th and 20th centuries. In the 1960s and 1970s, the feminist and civil rights movements sparked a renewed interest in Paganism and other alternative spiritualities. In the late 20th century, Paganism began to regain popularity in America. This resurgence was partly due to the growing awareness of environmental issues and the popularity of books and movies featuring pagan characters.

Paganism in Asia

Paganism is also practiced in many parts of Asia. In Japan, the native religion, Shinto, is a form of paganism. There are also many Pagans in China who practice Taoism, an indigenous Chinese religion with elements of Paganism. In India, there are numerous pagan traditions still practiced today. In Korea, shamanism is still practiced by a small minority of the population.

Paganism in Africa

It is often associated with ancient Egyptian religion and, more recently, with the traditional belief systems of the San people. However, there is no one African pagan tradition. Instead, there are a variety of pagan customs that are followed across the continent.

Africans believe that ancestors maintain spiritual connections with living relatives. There is a general tendency for ancestral spirits to be kind and good. Negative actions by ancestral spirits cause minor illnesses and warn people that they are erring on the wrong path.

San people, also known as Bushmen, are indigenous people of Southern Africa. The San follow a pagan religion based on animism, the belief that everything in nature has a spirit. Ancestors are considered powerful spirits who can help or harm the living.

Paganism in Australia and New Zealand

Paganism is also practiced in Australia and New Zealand. The most common type of Paganism in these countries is Wicca. The pagan religion of the Māori people is known as the Māori religion. As a form of animism, it holds that everything in nature is spiritual. It teaches that humans are connected to all things in nature and that people must respect and care for the natural world.

Paganism in the Indian Subcontinent

Paganism was also practiced in the Indian subcontinent, the most common type of Paganism being Hinduism. It is the oldest and most prominent religion in the subcontinent. It is a polytheistic religion, meaning Hindus believe in many gods and goddesses.

Paganism Today

Ever since the decline of Christianity in Europe, Paganism has greatly grown in popularity. As people became free to follow other belief systems, curiosity increased about past and distant cultures. This change began with the arrival of the Renaissance period around the middle of the 15th century. The first territory where shrines dedicated to pagan deities started to take off (besides Christian sites) was in Greece.

About a century later, Britain became a Protestant country, followed by the persecution of those who didn't follow this religion. After the upheaval ended, people were free to explore Non-Christian thoughts, including those from Greek and Roman literature describing tales and myths of pagan deities and heroes.

The first pagan belief system to be revived in Britain was Druidism. This was soon followed by other religions, as people continued to search for the fundamental principles of life by studying other religious beliefs from different places and times. In northern Europe, people rediscovered Anglo-Saxon and Norse Paganism.

Wicca, the newest form of Paganism, was developed in the late 19th century when there was a heightened interest in witchcraft among pagan practitioners. Wicca is loosely based on ancient pagan traditions but incorporates many modern elements. After the mid-20th century, other religious and spiritual traditions were similarly revived and incorporated into pagan practices.

One of the hallmarks of modern Paganism is the emphasis on feminism - likely the result of the feminist movement of the 1960s. The reverence of the single Great Goddess as the archetype of women's inner strength and dignity originates from this belief.

Pagan Religions

There are many different types of Paganism. The most common forms include Asatru, Heathenry, Druidism, Odinism, Animism, Celtic Reconstructionism, and Wicca. It's easy to see that Paganism represents a melting pot of different spiritual and religious beliefs. Each incorporates its own set of beliefs and traditions.

Animism relies on an age-old belief that everything in nature is imbued with spirit. This includes animals, plants, rocks, and even inanimate objects. Animism is one of the oldest religions in the world.

Druidism celebrates the Celtic pantheon of gods and goddesses. In ancient times, druids were the most class of the Celts. They were responsible for performing ceremonies, like making offerings and performing weddings and funerals. Druidism is an earth-based religion that emphasizes harmony with the natural world.

Wicca practitioners worship the goddesses of nature. They believe in the power of natural magic and use it to empower their spells and rituals. Wicca is one of the newest forms of the pagan religion.

Odinism is a type of Paganism revolving around worshiping the Norse gods, like Odin and Thor. Odinists believe in the power of magic and runes. They also place great importance on courage, honor, and loyalty.

Asatru is a form of Paganism venerating the Norse deities. It's similar to Odinism, except it emphasizes ethics and morality instead of magic.

Celtic Reconstructionists seek to revive the ancient Celtic culture and religion. They believe in following the traditional ways of their ancestors. They find it vital to preserve the ancient Celtic language and culture.

Heathenry relies on worshiping deities with Germanic pagan roots, like Odin and Thor. Its followers believe in magic and the power of runes. Their most prominent values are courage, honor, and loyalty.

The Core Beliefs of Paganism

Paganism is a polytheistic religion whose followers believe in multiple gods and goddesses. Each god or goddess represents a different aspect of the natural world or human experience. For example, there may be a god of the sun, a god of love, or a goddess of wisdom. Every aspect of the human experience was attributed to one or more of these gods and goddesses.

The divine as a concept also exists in several forms in Paganism. Some deities were attributed with feminine energies, while others had masculine energy. Many male pagan deities have female counterparts to maintain the natural balance. Some pagans also worship divinities embodying both feminine and masculine energies. The balance between feminine and masculine symbolizes fertility and procreation. Pagans equate this to the revival of the Earth at the beginning of each year on the pagan calendar.

They also believe in magic and the power of nature. They saw life as an ongoing cycle with birth, death, and rebirth - similar to how they saw the cyclical changes of nature. Pagans sought and still seek to live in peace with nature and strive to maintain a connection to it and respect it as much as possible.

Pagans follow no universal tenet. They aim to live in peace with themselves and those around them. They seek to avoid hurting others because they believe that any harm they cause can turn back against them.

Core Pagan Practices and Rituals

Pagan rituals and celebrations are often based on the changing of the seasons and the cycles of nature. They can also involve honoring deities or celebrating momentous occasions like birth, marriage, death, and transition into adulthood. While the method of celebration depends on traditions and personal preferences, pagans often engage in celebration both mentally and physically. Sacred rituals and festivities are often accompanied by dancing, singing, and drumming. The rites and ceremonies can include prayers and offerings, which can be in the form of objects, meals, and drinks. Offering these items to the ancestors or deities is believed to appease them and form a connection with them.

Pagans also use the representation of nature in their practices. Air, earth, water, and fire were often used in rituals, the consecration of items, or their cleansing. For example, taking a cleansing bath in salt water is a typical pagan way of preparing for rituals and ceremonies.

In ancient times, pagans often practiced in communities of various sizes. However, the number of solitary practitioners has increased significantly since the revival of Paganism. Pagans prefer to worship outdoors or in the sanctity of their homes - as long as they know they won't be disturbed. The primary reason for this lies in how most pagans commence their work. A typical pagan practice starts by focusing on one's mind, which requires grounding. A great way to achieve this is through meditation which connects the practitioner with nature's energy and allows them to maintain physical and emotional balance.

Building a shrine or an altar is also a common pagan practice. This represents a sacred space where pagans can address their deities and spiritual guides or enhance their spiritual practice. Pagans often erect shrines and altars in their homes, typically in the bedroom or other secluded areas. Those who live in rural settings and alone may create altars outdoors. Pagans decorate their altars with the representation of nature, their deities, beloved ancestors, objects of personal power, and magical tools. They can dedicate the altar to particular causes or entities, using it to leave offerings, meditate, perform cleansing or healing rituals, and much more.

It's unclear whether the ancient pagans performed other practices besides the ones that addressed deities, guides, and issues in their lives. However, modern pagans often do daily rituals as part of their spiritual practice. Nowadays, Paganism is considered a highly personal practice. One may choose to do a simple 10-minute meditation every day - while others will only celebrate sacred dates associated with seasonal changes or deities.

Pagan practices place a high emphasis on spoken intention. Many practitioners believe verbalizing their desires is the first step toward manifesting them. Because of this, pagans choose their words carefully during their practice to ensure they achieve their life goals.

Divination is another prevalent pagan practice. Different forms of Paganism rely on diverse divination methods and approaches - from asking what the day brings to inquiring about a specific future outcome. Tools used in divination include runes, Tarot cards, pendulums, animals, plants, and other elements of nature. Dreams can also be instruments of divination.

Some pagans wear sacred symbols, which serve as charms and talismans. One of the most well-known pagan symbols is the pentacle. It's considered a powerful symbol of protection, especially for those practicing magic. For pagans, magic is a spiritual practice that manifests changes, much like praying in other religions. The only difference is that magic has a physical component coupled with a clear intention. This conjunction enables the practitioner to boost their energy to support that intention. Pagans may choose to empower themselves through fierce concentration, chanting, or breathing methods. All of these exercises have the same goal: to release personal energy into whatever serves the practitioner's intention. Some practitioners use objects (like a candle or a charm) to harness the released power.

Anglo-Saxon Paganism and Norse Paganism

Anglo-Saxon and Norse Paganism are the two most widespread branches of ancient Germanic Paganism. They both stem from the same Proto-

Germanic pagan roots and have some similarities. For example, both the ancient Anglo-Saxon and Norse pagans worshiped the same deities and had similar views on ancestral worship and reverence for nature. However, they were two distinct religions. Their diversified evolution began soon after the Germanic pagan tribes migrated and settled in different parts of Europe. As soon as the Anglo Saxon tribes invaded the territory of Great Britain, they started to develop local traditions. The names and functions of their deities may have changed, and other gods and goddesses were added to their pantheon. Their written language (the runic alphabet) was changed, and additional staves were added. The Norse pagans, on the other hand, settled in Scandinavia and maintained most of their original Germanic traditions. This included the names and roles of their gods and goddesses, places and methods of worship, and the original set of rune staves. The evolution of Anglo-Saxon Paganism was cut short around the 7th century when the tribes were forcibly converted to Christianity. Norse Paganism continued to evolve until the 12th century because pagans in Scandinavia and central Europe converted to Christianity much later. After their conversion, the former Anglo-Saxon pagans adopted many Christian traditions, whereas Norse pagans maintained some of their core traditions. Because of all these differences, the Norse pagan belief system has been far better preserved throughout history than its Anglo-Saxon counterpart.

Chapter 2: Norse Religion: Old and Modern

Norse Paganism heavily relies on ancient Norse lore, tying religion and mythology closely together. This chapter will introduce you to the Norse religion in two parts. First, it will explore the Old Norse myths and beliefs, and it will then show you how the Norse religion has evolved in modern times.

The Old Norse Religion

The earliest evidence of Norse religion comes from the Iron Age. Archeological evidence of motifs of sun worship, as wheel crosses from the Iron Age Scandinavia, indicate that a nature-based religion existed at the time. The Norse religion developed from a much older Germanic Iron Age religion. Evidence from the early days of the Norse religion is sparse. However, after the Scandinavian tribes left their home territories and settled in other parts of Northwestern Europe, they spread their belief system. For example, when the Norse tribes arrived in Norway, they brought their god Thor, the most popular deity among the common Norse people.

Up until the arrival of Christianity, Norse Paganism was flourishing in Europe. The British tribes were the first to convert to the new religion. And when Christianity reached Scandinavia, it was already a prominent religion in Europe. However, the Scandinavian pagans were much slower to convert. While the conversion brought many benefits to European kings, the commoners wanted to remain faithful to their ancient traditions and beliefs. One of the reasons for the resistance was the polytheistic nature of the Norse religion. When mass conversion became the norm, many followers of the Norse religion simply absorbed the Christian god as another deity into their faith. Christianity inadvertently inspired new forms of pagan expressions by influencing various myths.

By the 12th century, Christianity had spread to all corners of Northwestern Europe, nearly eradicating all other religions from these areas, including Norse Paganism. However, the stories of the mighty Norse deities continued to be passed down orally for at least two centuries. While it's unclear how the transmission occurred, some believe the Norse gods were worshipped in secrecy by faithful devotees who were hesitant to abandon their pagan past. As a result, Norse mythology remained popular for hundreds of years after belief in its deities had faded. Despite the prevalence of Christianity in Scandinavia during this period, pagan rituals were observed for centuries afterward. Today, Norse mythology is still important to many people and is a source of inspiration in art, literature, and music.

The Norse Belief System

The ancient Norse religion was polytheistic and concentrated on the reverence of a pantheon of gods, goddesses, and other supernatural beings.

Norse Deities

The ancient Norse were divided into two tribes; the Aesir and the Vanir. The Aesir were the first tribe of gods, living in the heavens and attributed with celestial powers. Living in Asgard, they ruled over war, wisdom, courage, and duty. They were worshiped by warriors and leaders. The Aesir were protectors who watched over the other kingdoms and established law and order across all the realms. The Vanir, on the other hand, were minor gods and goddesses associated with the natural world. Living in Vanaheim, the Vanir were deities of fertility, harvest, the sea, seasons, and love. The followers were peasants who depended more on nature's cycles.

The Aesir Gods

Odin

Odin, god of magic and wisdom.[10]

Odin was the most powerful and feared of the Norse gods. Not only was he respected by mortals but also by the gods. He was the god of wisdom, magic, war, and poetry. However, despite being a symbol of justice, he was also known for disguising himself and stirring trouble among the mortals, which often led to wars. According to the lore, he did this to collect the warriors' souls in Valhalla and build an army for the upcoming battle at Ragnarok.

Odin also was considered to be a god of shamanism and had a significant influence on shamans. According to the Old Norse legends, he could travel to other realms while seemingly looking asleep or dead. Odin had two ravens that brought him news from all the realms and two wolves that served as his loyal and fierce companions.

Odin has often been associated with poetry in Norse myths and has been known to speak eloquently and use poems in his speech. Poetry, or in other words, knowledge, was a gift he carried and gave only to those he deemed worthy. Odin stole the mead of poetry from the giants and gave it to the gods and goddesses of his choosing, along with a few mortal followers.

Odin is associated with death. As an avid seeker of knowledge, he was known for his ability to communicate with the dead. Some sources suggest that he even raised the souls of the dead to seek their knowledge and wisdom.

Frigg

As the most powerful of the Aesir goddesses and Odin's wife, Frigg is the queen of Asgard. For the Germanic people, Frigg was a symbol of motherhood, although her roles were diminished in Norse mythology. She is also the patron goddess of marriage, and the day Friday was derived from her name. Therefore, Norse Pagans believed that Friday was the best day to get married. While some sources depict Frigg as unfaithful or cunning, she was shown in the Poetic Edda to be a loving mother and wife. She wept when her son Baldur was killed. She was always mentioned as Odin's equal and a worthy match for him regarding wisdom and intellect.

Thor

As the protector and guardian of warriors, Thor was one of the most prominent figures in the Aesir pantheon. He believed in order and was the god people turned to when they wanted social stability and justice. Thor was the god of thunder and the sky and, in some versions of the Norse myths, of agriculture. He was birthed by Jord, the embodiment of the Earth and one of Odin's lovers.

Thor was the defender of Asgard and Midgard, a mighty warrior and a masculine figure whose legend continued over the years and passed from generation to generation. There are several myths of him slaying giants to defend either world. While his compelling sense of duty often put him in danger, he never relented in his efforts to protect the weak and those who needed his help. His faithful companion - his hammer Mjöllnir - was his largest weapon, but he also used it for other purposes. For example, he used it to bless weddings, social events, and lands where peasants would plant crops or build their dwellings.

According to the lore, Thor travels across Asgard and Midgard in a chariot pulled by two goats. He is also associated with rain and tidal waves and was asked to bless crops and help people find sustenance. He is said to be straightforward but often only follows his own moral compass. Thor was prophesied to die in Ragnarok, but he would do this by first taking down the world serpent, Jörmungandr.

Loki

Loki is a trickster god in Norse mythology, notorious for mischief and crime. His position in the Aesir pantheon isn't entirely clear. While most sources claim his father to be Jotunn Farbauti and his mother the giantesses Laufey, other sources disagree. Loki is often depicted as Thor and Odin's companion, but he most likely used them for his own gain. Often self-serving and disregarding the consequences of his actions, Loki is usually described as a deity who does what he wants.

Despite this, Loki also used his wit and cunning several times to help his companion gods escape trouble. He was also known for making things right and fixing whatever he ruined, although doing this sometimes under duress. Because of his intellect, the Aesir often calls on Loki to help solve problems, even when it isn't his fault.

Loki is a shapeshifter who can change form and gender - evidenced by the fact that he mothered some of his children and fathered others. His offspring play a pivotal role in Ragnarok, as two would kill the Aesir's most powerful warriors, Odin and Thor. Loki and Heimdall are predicted to battle during Ragnarok, and the two will kill one another. Perhaps the most notorious tale of Loki's mischief in Norse myths is how he had Baldur killed through deception - and later on, continued with his scheme and stopped the return of Baldur's soul from Hel.

Baldur

The Aesir god of ineffable wisdom, Baldur, was also known for his striking features. He settled disputes among feuding gods and mortals - and did this using only his charm and wit. As a son of Odin, Baldur had many brothers and half-brothers, including Thor. He wed the goddess Nanna, and their son Forseti inherited his father's wisdom and appreciation for justice. He resolved conflict in the same calm manner and was known to be a symbol of peace and justice.

Heimdall

As the guardian of the Aesir realm of Asgard, Heimdall lived in Himinbjorg. Ever watchful and vigilant, Heimdall was blessed with hearing so powerful that he could listen to the grass growing and wool growing on sheep. He could also see for hundreds of miles, day and night.

Heimdall was one of Odin's sons and is another figure held in high regard by the Norse Pagans and other Germanic people. Some sources claim him to be the father of mankind, possibly because he taught mortals many things, like the notion of social classes. When he wasn't standing guard, Heimdall wandered Midgard in disguise, advising people, especially couples. Some sources suggest that Heimdall was born to nine maidens, who were also sisters. He wielded a massive sword, and according to some tales, he had the gift of foresight and could look into the future.

Tyr

Tyr is one of the oldest gods in Germanic lore, associated with war, peace, treaties, and justice. Unlike Odin, who only incited wars, Tyr was tied to all aspects of battle, including its ending. His name is associated with the day "Tuesday," which connects to the two names, Tyr and Mars - the latter stemming from Tyr's adoption by Romans as their god Mars.

Tyr was responsible for upholding order and law as well as spreading justice. He was also courageous. This was shown in the tale of the binding of Fenrir, where Tyr sacrificed his arm to ensure that the giant beast was bound and could not hurt anyone. His sacrifice is often compared to that of Odin, who sacrificed his eye to gain knowledge.

The Vanir Gods

Freyja

Fathered by Njord, Freyja was born to the Vanir tribe on Vanaheim until she was kidnapped and taken to Asgard after the war, where she lived among the Aesir. She was married to her brother Freyr. Freyja is often associated with love, lust, fertility, and beauty. It is said that her beauty was unparalleled, and all who saw her coveted her. She was fond of her attributes and liked to indulge in pleasure and passion.

Freyja was also a skilled magic practitioner and heavily associated with shamanism and Seidr. Because of this, she was considered a seeress among the gods. She had many shamanic and magical powers, like transforming into a falcon. According to some Norse tales, she was associated with war and battle. She claimed half the souls of fallen warriors in the battle for her realm Folkvangr.

Freyr

Freyja's brother Freyr was another fertility god in Norse mythology, and he's been linked to the sun and abundance. Freyr was one of the most prominent gods among the Vanir tribe and was worshiped more than his sister or father. After he and his sister departed from the Vanir, Freyr is believed to have been married to the Jotunn Gerðr, another goddess. Freyr was also a valiant warrior who was not without battlefield experience. He's prophesied to fight the fire giant Surtr in Ragnarok and die.

Freyr was often prayed to as a fertility god for a successful harvest. He could control the rain and sunshine, and mortals asked for his blessing so they could prosper. Freyr was linked to masculinity and was invoked in weddings and social celebrations to bring happiness. He was also loved by the gods because he blessed them with abundance during harvest, wealth, and fertility.

Njord

Njord was the father of Freyja and Freyr and the Vanir god of hunting, fishing, seafaring, and the wind. Like many Vanir Gods, he was also associated with fertility and wealth. After the war, he was sent to Asgard along with Freyja and Freya, making him an honorary member of the Aesir.

Norse Mythology and Cosmology

Norse mythology starts with the myth of creation and ends with Ragnarok - the end of the world and the death of most gods and mortals. According to Norse beliefs, the creation of the world started with Ginnungagap, a giant gap that existed even before the sea, land, or sky was formed.

This was located between the realm of ice, Niflheim, and the realm of fire, Muspelheim. The latter was filled with molten lava and smoke, and when the fires leaped out of it, they clashed with the ice growing out from Niflheim. As a result, in Ginnungagap, the fire melted the ice, and out of the drops of melted ice came Ymir, the first giant. The melted drops also created Audhumla (Auðumbla), the primeval cow whose milk nourished Ymir. When Ymir slept, giants were born out of his arms and legs. Auðumbla survived by licking salty rime rocks for nourishment, which is how the first Aesir god, Buri, was created. His son Bor wed Bestla, the daughter of the giant Bolthorn, and from their union, Odin, Vili, and Ve were born.

The three brothers went on to shape the world. Odin, Vili, and Ve killed Ymir and took his body to Ginnungagap. There, they used his blood to flood the abyss, forming the oceans. They used his skin and muscles to make the soil, while his hair was used to create vegetation. They used Ymir's bones shaped rocks and stones and his brain to form the clouds, after placing his skull over the Earth to form the sky out of it. The brothers then used the embers of Muspelheim to make light and stars. Odin, Vili, and Ve created the first man and woman from tree trunks. They called them Ask and Embla.

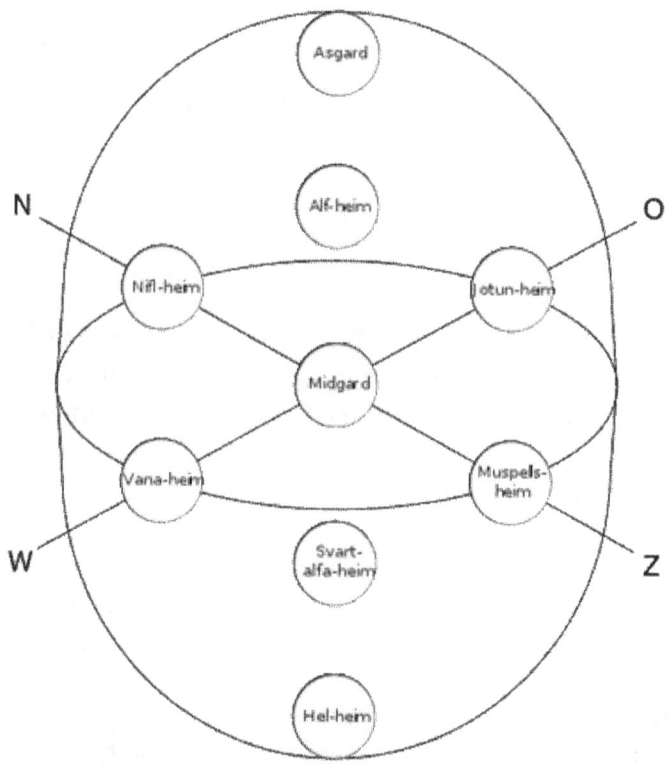

The nine realms.[11]

In Norse mythology, the universe consists of nine realms connected by the World Tree Yggdrasil. The nine realms are:

- **Asgard:** The home of the Aesir gods and goddesses.
- **Vanaheim:** The world where the Vanir gods and goddesses lived.
- **Midgard:** The world of mortals.
- **Muspelheim:** The primordial world of fire.
- **Niflheim:** The primordial world of ice.
- **Jotunheim:** The world of the frost giants.
- **Nidavellir or Svartalfheim:** The home of the dwarves.
- **Alfheim:** The world of the light elves.
- **Hel or Helheim:** The underworld.

The Norse Religion's Core Values

Animism

Norse Pagans didn't look for the divine energies in the sky but in everyday life and everything surrounding them. According to myth, the deities didn't always dwell in a distant realm. Instead, they took the form of animals and other aspects of nature. Spirits and magic were found in even inanimate objects, like rocks.

The Importance of Ancestors

Norse Pagans deeply revered their ancestors and took great pride in keeping in touch with them. Ancestors were part of the family, and a strong connection with them could provide plenty of benefits. Those who disregard their heritage and their ancestors are believed to be destined to experience many misfortunes.

Hospitality, Hard Work, and Integrity

The ancient Norse people cared deeply for social values, integrity, and order. They found it just as necessary to be gracious hosts as they did to work hard to achieve their goals. They believed that you could only save your integrity if you remained productive and sought to live in peace in your community.

Fate

A powerful belief in fate was a pillar of Norse Pagan traditions, as it was believed that none could escape it, not even the gods.

However, despite having events that were predestined, the Norse also believed in being in control of their actions. They didn't let their belief in the power of fate take away their free will. The warriors often chose to embrace death with honor because they believed it to be a measure of their character and honor.

Spiritual Practices

Most Norse pagan practices revolve around ancestor worship and reverence of deities. Both groups are offered sacrifices and prayers in the hope of receiving blessings. Creating burial mounds for the dead was an accepted practice of the Norse pagans, with the size and shape of the mound determining the status of the deceased.

The Blot is a type of sacrifice often seen as part of private or public spiritual practices of the Norse pagans. It involved killing animals (and, according to some sources, humans) and offering their blood and organs to the deities or ancestors.

Norse Pagan spiritual practices sometimes also involved using divination and magic. Runic divination stemmed from the ancient Germanic culture and was widely used among Norse Pagans in ancient times and even today. The most prominent magical practice is Seidr, a unique form of shamanism initially practiced by Freyja and Odin.

The Importance of the Afterlife

The Norse people believed in the afterlife. They assumed that after leaving the body, the souls of the departed traveled to the otherworld. The spirits ended up in one of the five spiritual realms thought by the Norse people to have existed.

The Modern Revival

Nowadays, people still practice Norse Paganism to connect with their ancestors and honor the cycles of life, death, and rebirth. By honoring and connecting with their ancestors through rituals, teachings, and communal gatherings, followers of modern Norse Paganism can gain a deeper understanding and appreciation of life. Whether by participating in traditional Norse ceremonies or simply by taking time each day to connect with nature, they better understand how to honor the past.

Heathenism

Also known as Heathenry, Heathenism centers on the pantheon of the Germanic pagans. Its beliefs and practices include animism and honoring the deities in ancestors in blots, alongside serving food and alcoholic beverages. Lead by the desire to acquire wisdom and guidance from the Norse divinities. Some followers embark on the path of Seidr. Some are solitary practitioners, while others gather in small groups to perform Heathen rituals and ceremonies outdoors or in sacred places of worship. Their primary values are personal integrity, loyalty, and honor. Beliefs about the afterlife are rarely part of a Heathen's work.

Vanatru

Like the name (translated as */true to the Vanir')* indicates, Vanatru is dedicated to the Vanir tribe of the Norse deities. The practitioners' belief centers on fertility, divination, and magic. They treat the gods and goddesses of the Vanir tribe as mortals instead of divine beings. They honor and respect them and expect honor and respect in return. With Vanatru, there are different ways to invoke certain gods and goddesses in rituals, and offerings are made to them.

Rökkatru

Followers of Rökkatru do not see bad events as consequences of evil forces, not even death. For them, chaos, death, and random destructive parts of nature are all necessary to keep the balance of the universe. They don't believe in dividing the deities into "good" and "bad" either. All gods and goddesses are worthy of honor and should be equally celebrated.

Asatru

This is the most widespread branch of modern Norse Paganism. The term Asatru can be translated as 'true to the Aesir gods,' which indicates that the beliefs followed center on the Aiser deities. They worship deities like Odin, Thor, and Baldur. Unlike in ancient times when animal sacrifices were common offerings, today, devotees usually drink mead or other beverages as a homage to the gods or share a meal with them. The practitioners of Asatru embrace nature and value life, and they are on a constant journey searching for harmony.

Chapter 3: The Asatru Religion

Asatru is pronounced as "OW-sa-troo," meaning *"to be true to the Aesir."* It is derived from the ancient Norse word *"oss,"* which is the singular of Aesir, and the word *"tru,"* which translates to faith. Although ancient Norse beliefs influenced the religion, the term "Asatru" is considered modern and only came into use in the 19th century.

Asatru is a neo-pagan belief that reconstructs and revises the ancient Norse religion. It is a polytheistic belief that involves the worship of more than one deity, and its followers are called heathens or Ásatrúar (singular and plural). However, they prefer not to use the term "neopagans" since their religion shares many similarities to the Norse "Old Way." Many neo-pagan beliefs are based on new and old traditions, unlike Asatru, which solely focuses on old traditions inspired by surviving ancient records.

Although many deities exist in the Asatru pantheon, it mainly focuses on Odin, Thor, Loki, Heimdall, Baldur, Frig, Freyja, Tyr, and Freyr. The religion also involves the worship of giants and ancestors, the spirits of honorable and brave individuals who impacted the people and society while they were alive.

This chapter will dive into the world of the Asatru religion and cover its history, beliefs, practices, symbols, and seasonal festivals.

The History of the Asatru

Sveinbjörn Beinteinsson, Asatru high priest.[12]

Before Christianity arrived in Europe, most of the continent followed different pagan religions. Iceland was introduced to Asatru after many of the religion's practitioners moved to the country in the 900s. It spread rapidly and became one of the main religions in the country. However, things changed in the year 1000 after Christianity eradicated all pagan beliefs, including Asatru, and became the country's official religion. There were still people who held onto their ancient beliefs and who practiced Asatru in secret.

The pagan religion faded into obscurity until 1973 when Sveinbjörn Beinteinsson, a farmer who later became an Asatru high priest, decided to bring it back. One day in 1972, Beinteinsson met with three of his friends Þorsteinn Guðjónsson, Dagur Þorleifsson, and Jörmundur Ingi Hansen, who would all later become influential figures of Asatru, in a coffee house in Reykjavík, the capital of Iceland. After an interesting conversation, the four men agreed to revive the ancient pagan belief. The cultural environment of Iceland at the time, the nationalist movement, and the interest in spiritual beliefs made them realize that the people of Iceland were ready to be reacquainted with the religion of their ancestors.

Sveinbjörn Beinteinsson felt that Asatru was specifically connected to Iceland since it was influenced by the land's hidden forces. He also believed that the people wanted a religion reflecting their identity and would most likely rally behind an ancient belief more than imported religions like Christianity. People were also starting to notice the negative impact of the industrial movement and its ugly side and wanted to return to nature. Beinteinsson found that these elements also created the perfect opportunity to bring back Asatru.

Sveinbjörn Beinteinsson and Þorsteinn Guðjónsson embarked on their journey to resurrect it and spread its beliefs. They wanted to get Asatru recognized as one of the country's official religions. In December 1972, they met with Ólafur Jóhannesson, the country's minister of ecclesiastical affairs and justice. When the men presented their idea, the minister thought they were playing a prank or joking and didn't take them seriously. However, they explained that they were serious and wanted to take this step immediately, so the minister requested they bring him all the necessary paperwork.

Interestingly, after the men left the minister's office, a thunderstorm hit Reykjavík, causing the lights to go out in various areas around the city. The press at the time made a joke that Thor was expressing his anger since he wasn't pleased with the minister's reaction to Beinteinsson and Guðjónsson.

When Asatru began gaining recognition among the people of Iceland, it faced opposition from various Christian leaders and, more precisely, Sigurbjörn Einarsson, the bishop of Iceland. He expressed his disapproval in an Icelandic newspaper and explained that although their constitution allowed people to create religious institutions, they were intended to be monotheistic and only serve one God. He also attacked them for not having a house of worship which is unorthodox for any religious belief and criticized their vague teachings.

The bishop wanted to alienate people even further from Asatru, so he connected its main beliefs to those of Nazi Germany and accused them of having the same ideologies. He put into question Asatru's moral background as well. He added that since it only had twenty-one followers, it didn't need to be recognized as a religious organization. The press echoed the priest's sentiments and declared Christianity as the only Icelandic religion and that they didn't need another faith.

The members of Asatru defended their religion against these attacks and fought even harder for it to be recognized. Their efforts didn't go in vain, and in 1973, the government finally accepted it as an official Icelandic religion. This gave them the right to perform various ceremonies, including marriages. After Iceland, Denmark, and Norway recognized Asatru as an official religion, it reached the UK and USA.

It spread throughout the country to become Iceland's most common and fast-growing religion. However, their priests didn't feel the need to approach people and convince them to join their faith. They believed that their ceremonies and religious teachings would be enough to draw people to Asatru.

Asatru Main Beliefs

What makes any religion unique is its main beliefs. Although ancient Norse mythology glorified wars and made heroes of its soldiers, Asatru's beliefs are different. It promotes peace and tolerance and advises its followers to avoid bloodshed and fighting. The religion also focuses on finding harmony and being connected with nature. Unlike Christianity, Judaism, and other religions, Asatru doesn't have a set of principles or scripture that people should follow.

Another aspect that sets them apart is how they view their gods and goddesses. They didn't treat them as perfect beings. In fact, they are all flawed and have weaknesses and human qualities. They can fall in love, feel hate, get angry, sad, jealous, etc. Asatru practitioners don't pray to their gods and goddesses and see them more as friends than superiors. However, they believe they play a significant role in their daily lives.

Although Asatru doesn't have religious scriptures, it is highly influenced by the Prose Edda by Snorri Sturluson. In fact, many of their beliefs are inspired by the many ancient myths from these texts.

There is usually one high priest who leads the Asatru organization and who is referred to as Allsherjargoði, and ten other minor priests supervise congregations all over the country. The goði of kjalarnesþing is the second highest ranking position in the Asatru hierarchy, and they have the power to perform blót, funerals, marriages, and other religious ceremonies.

The Nine Noble Virtues of Asatru

Although Asatru doesn't follow a set of rules, its worshipers are governed by specific guidelines called "The Nine Noble Virtues." They are a collection of ethical and moral standards that all followers of Asatru must abide by to lead an honorable life. These virtues are based on the Poetic Prose Edda, the Havamal poem, and various Icelandic sagas. Each branch of Asatru has its own interpretation of the nine virtues, but their basics and universal meaning are the same.

Perseverance

Perseverance is the virtue of the strong. No matter what obstacles one faces, one should never give up and must keep going. However, this quality doesn't only involve getting up on your feet every time you face defeat but also learning from your bad decisions and mistakes and becoming a better version of yourself.

Living an average or mediocre life is easy, but success requires perseverance and achieving your full potential. You should never let life bring you down, especially when you feel that all the doors are closed, or there is no hope. Perseverance is believing that nothing is impossible.

Self-Reliance

Self-reliance is being independent and taking care of your needs while remaining connected to the gods and goddesses. Although you should honor your deities regularly, you shouldn't ignore your own well-being and spend time nourishing your heart, mind, body, and soul. Asatru practitioners establish this balance by helping others and doing good deeds without sacrificing their own needs. In Asatru, a community can only thrive and flourish if individuals have room to grow and become better people.

Industriousness

Industriousness is working hard to make your dreams a reality and accomplish your goals. This involves your job and your relationships with deities, community, and family. Think of your Viking ancestors and how people lived their lives. These people were warriors and hard workers who never slacked or wouldn't have survived. Their family would go hungry if they didn't go out looking for food. Although you don't need to exert the same effort to survive, Asatru practitioners believe that one should always have a goal to work toward and keep their mind and body busy. However, you should give yourself a break every now and then, or you'll burn out and won't keep going.

Hospitality

Most people define hospitality as graciously welcoming people into your home. However, Asatru urges its followers to also treat others with love and respect even if they aren't guests. Community is a big part of the faith, and one should learn to coexist peacefully with others. This is a trait they acquired from their ancestors, as hospitality was more than just being polite and nice. In fact, their survival depended on it. Communities should welcome strangers and travelers looking for companionship, safety, and shelter. According to Asatru tradition, if you welcome a stranger into your home and serve them food, you must keep them safe as long as they are your guests. This was based on verses from the Havamal poem.

Honor

Honor involves having a moral compass and maintaining a good reputation. This virtue impacts every aspect of the lives of the Asatru followers. It serves as a reminder that even when your body perishes, your reputation, actions, deeds, words, and how you treat others will never be forgotten.

Truth

According to the Havamal poem, there are two types of truth; the actual truth and the spiritual truth. One of its verses cautions against making an oath unless one plans to keep it, or one will encounter severe punishment. Truth is one of the most significant and powerful virtues. It reminds you to be honest rather than being a people pleaser and say what others want.

Courage

One can't think of the Vikings without the word "courage" coming to mind. This virtue involves being physically and morally brave, *but not just in battle*. One should have the courage to stand up for what is right, even if the whole world is against them. In fact, it takes guts to live by these nine virtues, especially in the modern world. However, you should always be yourself and follow your heart and beliefs, no matter what.

Fidelity

Fidelity isn't only being faithful to your partner but also to the deities and your community. In ancient Norse paganism, an oath was sacred, and breaking it was considered disgraceful. If you break your oath to the gods, family, friends, or spouse, you are letting down your community and turning your back on its principles.

Discipline

Discipline has the willpower to lead an honorable life while upholding these virtues. Nowadays, with the many temptations people face regularly, having morals and holding on to them requires a lot of discipline. You can choose to live your life by these virtues or ignore them and follow the masses. Discipline is being loyal to your morals and brave against the daily challenges you face in the modern world.

All these virtues are connected; failing to adhere to one will also impact the other virtues.

Asatru Practices

Most of the Asatru communities in Iceland remain true to the lifestyle of their Viking ancestors. Ever since the religion's resurrection in 1973, its various practices have spread across the nation.

Offerings

One of the most popular practices in Asatru involves honoring the ancestors. Worshipers usually go to specific sacred sites like an ancient Viking ship or an ancient burial mound to present offerings to the spirits of their dearly departed.

Invoking Deities

A male priest (Gode) or a female priestess (Gydje) usually leads this ceremony. They form a circle with other worshipers to create a sacred space that acts as a portal to the heavens where their gods and goddesses reside. They then invoke and venerate a specific deity and make offerings to appease them. They usually perform this ceremony during the four seasonal festivals; autumn equinox, summer solstice, spring solstice, and winter solstice.

Symbols of Asatru

Many Asatru symbols originate from ancient Norse pagan beliefs dating back to 2000 B.C.

Mjölnir

Thanks to Marvel movies, many people are familiar with Mjölnir. Thor's powerful and magical hammer is one of the oldest Norse symbols. In ancient belief, worshipers wore it as a pendant. It symbolizes community, protection, blessings, good fortune, growth, and fertility.

Yggdrasil

Yggdrasil represents the cycle of life.[18]

Yggdrasil is one of the most important symbols in Asatru and Norse mythology. It represents the cycle of life and connects all living things together. The tree stands at the center of the universe, and all the realms exist on its roots. The word "Yggdrasil" means "Odin's horse" since it was where Odin bound it. According to Norse mythology, Yggdrasil will be destroyed at the end of the world, which is referred to as Ragnarok.

Triskelion

Triskelion means Odin's horns, and they represent poetic inspiration and wisdom.

Huginn and Muninn

Huginn and Muninn were Odin's ravens, symbolizing memory and thought. After any battle, the ravens would feed on the dead bodies, and they treated this event as a feast. This is similar to Odin feasting with the spirits of the dead heroes in Valhalla.

Valknut

Valknut means "Odin's knot," representing the process of life and death. It also symbolizes the spirits of the dead heroes who fell in battle and entered Valhalla.

Aegishjalmur

Aegishjalmur means frightening helmet, and it is the helmet of Aegir, the god of the sea. It represents protection and power. Soldiers used to engrave pictures of it on their weapons or armor since it could terrorize the enemy and make it much easier to defeat them.

Seasonal Festivals of Asatru

Asatru followers have a festival for every season, and each one has its own celebrations.

Yule/Winter Solstice (20th December)

Yule takes place during the winter, derived from the ancient Norse word "Hjol," which means "wheel." During this festival, people celebrate by throwing feasts, dancing, and exchanging gifts. It is one of the most sacred and significant holidays since it symbolizes the return of Baldur, the god of beauty and light from Hel, to ease the grip of the freezing winter. This is a magical time when the gods and goddesses are close to Earth, and the spirits of the dead are able to cross and roam among the living.

Even though Yule shares many similarities with Christmas, it predates the Christian holiday for thousands of years.

Fall Feast/Autumn Equinox (September 21st)

This festival takes place at the beginning of the fall. People celebrate it by dancing, feasting, and lighting bonfires. It symbolizes harvesting fruit and vegetables and storing them for the winter.

Midsummer/Summer Solstice (June 21st)

This festival takes place on the longest day of the year. People celebrate it by singing, dancing, making speeches, lighting bonfires, and presenting offerings to Baldur.

Ostara/Spring Equinox (March 21st)

This festival is named after Ostara, the goddess of spring. It is a time to celebrate the Earth's fertility and growth. People celebrate it by decorating their homes and painting eggs. Ostara greatly influences the Easter Christian holiday, celebrated with the same traditions.

Asatru is a fascinating religion with a rich history and various beliefs and practices. It has remained faithful to the Norse Old Way, for the most part. Asatru still uses the same ancient religion's symbols, follows similar core beliefs, and celebrates the same seasonal festivals.

Chapter 4: The Soul and the Afterlife

Death has always been the biggest mystery in life. Even though people know they are going to die, they don't know where their souls will end up or what happens in the afterlife. Since the beginning of time, mankind has been trying to answer the question, "What happens after you die?" Ancient Norse mythology came up with its own interpretation of the soul and the afterlife to turn death into something people can look forward to rather than fear.

This chapter discusses the concept of the soul and the afterlife and their significance in Norse religion.

The Afterlife in Norse Religion

Death and the afterlife are some of the most significant concepts in Norse mythology. However, there are a lot of misunderstandings about these topics thanks to the media's inaccurate portrayals of the Vikings. For instance, many people believe that Valhalla is similar to the idea of heaven in many religions. However, it is quite different from that.

Most religions focus on the afterlife and advise their followers to lead honest and decent lives so they can spend eternity in heaven. However, the Norse religion focuses more on life experiences and enjoyment instead of worrying about where a person will end up after they die. In other words, people's actions are only connected to their well-being and sense of fulfillment and have no impact on where their souls will go. This is clear in the nine virtues that only focus on improving the individual and the community. There is no mention that following those nine virtues will allow people entry to Valhalla. The Norse believed that every person is granted an afterlife eventually, so there is no need to worry about it.

Valhalla, the hall of the slain.[14]

Death isn't seen as the end but as a continuation of one's life in a different realm and state of being. The soul departs the body and goes to the world of the dead to continue its existence. However, it remains connected to the mortal world, which is why the living and spirits of the ancestors can communicate with one another.

Spirits don't all end up in the same place. There is more than one afterlife, and there are factors that determine where each spirit will spend eternity.

Valhalla

If you have ever watched a Viking movie or TV show, you have probably heard the word Valhalla. It means *"hall of the slain,"* and it is the place where the Valkyries take the souls of fallen heroes after they die. The Valkyries resemble their deception in the Marvel movies. They are a group of warrior women who ride on boars, wolves, or horses, holding a spear to determine the fate of the warriors who fall in battle.

The Grímnismál, one of the poems from the Poetic Edda, describes Valhalla as a bright gold place with a roof made of shields and rafters made of spears. The dead sit on chairs covered with breastplates around enormous feasting tables that serve an endless supply of food and drinks like meat and mead. They spend all day training by fighting one another, and at night, all their scars and injuries heal, and they eat delicious food while surrounded by beautiful Valkyries.

According to Norse mythology, Loki's son *Fenrir* is a monstrous wolf who is so huge and vicious that the gods had to put him in chains. During Ragnarok (the end of the world in Norse mythology), Fenrir would break free and wreak havoc on the nine realms, and he would fight Odin and then kill him. For this reason, the gods collect the souls of dead warriors and train them to fight Fenrir.

Valhalla is different from the concept of heaven most people are accustomed to since it doesn't represent the ideal afterlife. However, for a Viking warrior, nothing is better than spending their days fighting and feasting. Still, Odin didn't create Valhalla as a reward for the warriors. It was for selfish reasons since he was aware of Ragnarok and wanted to prepare an army to protect him when the time came.

The warriors won't spend eternity in Valhalla. They are all destined to die again with all the other gods during Ragnarok. Then, they will perish forever.

Fólkvangr

Fólkvangr means field of the armies or field of the people, and it is the realm of Freyja, the goddess of war and death. The souls of fallen warriors are divided between Odin and Freya, half going to Valhalla and the other going to Fólkvangr. There is no mention in Grímnismál about which factors determine who ends up in Valhalla and who ends up in Fólkvangr.

There also isn't any description of Fólkvangr or how the spirits there spend their days. It only mentions how fair and great it is. However, one can expect that it is a nice place to spend the afterlife since Freyja is a kind and giving goddess, so her realm would most likely reflect her loving personality.

Hel

Hel or Helheim is a realm named after its queen, Hel, the goddess of death. The word "Hel" means hidden, and it reflects how the dead and their realm are hidden deep underground. It is a misty, cold, dark, and damp place with a dog guarding its gates. The Poetic Edda states that the goddess is the daughter of Loki and Fenrir's sister. Being a part of one of the most dangerous families in Norse mythology is reflected in her personality. She is a harsh, cruel, and greedy goddess and doesn't care about the dead or the living.

People who die of diseases, old age, or accidents end up in her realm. However, the Prose Edda hints that those who die from other causes could also end up there. When Baldur, the god of light, was murdered at the hands of his brother, he went to Hel. However, one could argue that it could be considered an accident since his brother didn't kill him on purpose (Loki tricked him).

Unlike the goddess's name and personality suggest, Hel isn't a bad place, and the spirits aren't tortured or punished. In fact, she treats them very well. When Baldur died, the goddess welcomed him by covering the floor with gold. However, Hel isn't similar to the concept of heaven since it is neither a pleasant place nor a bad one. It is simply a realm for the dead to spend their days until Ragnarok. They would eat, drink, sleep, and live just like when they were alive.

Some scholars believe that Snorri was the only one to portray Hel negatively since most Norse literature described it as a rather pleasant place. They also believe that he contradicted himself when he mentioned that Baldur went to Hel since there is no mention that people who were murdered ended up there.

From all this information, one can gather that Hel is indeed a good place where the dead have everything they want.

The Realm of Rán

This realm is located under the sea and is the afterlife for those who die by drowning. The goddess of the sea, Rán, rules over it, and when sailors drown, she takes their souls to her world. Even though it is located under the sea, her realm is usually illuminated by all the treasures she takes from the sunken ships. It is believed that Rán treats the spirits well and looks after them.

Helgafjell

Helgafjell is a holy mountain where some spirits spend their afterlife. It is similar to Hel, where the dead lead normal lives with their families and loved ones. Some people have the power to see into Helgafjell, and they describe it as a joyful place that feels like home.

The Burial Mound

The burial mound isn't a realm but the grave where a person is buried. Sometimes, the soul remains in the tombs and spends the afterlife there. The soul is free to dwell in peace or haunt the town and scare the people.

There is no mention that a person's actions impact where they will spend their afterlife. The only determining factor is how they died. The concepts of salvation or internal damnation don't exist in Norse religions. There is only one mention in Norse literature of a place resembling "Hell," called Nastrond, but Christian ideologies mainly influence the belief in this scenario.

The gods don't judge a person based on their deeds or actions, nor do they have the power to interfere with where the souls go. For instance, Odin couldn't take the soul of a person who died by drowning, and Rán couldn't take that of one who died in battle.

The Self in Norse Religion

The self consists of the soul, mind, and body. Simply put, they are the components that make a human being; without one, a person will perish. In Norse mythology, the concept of the self is more complex. It consists of other parts that can be separated from one another. Some of these components can still live on when a person dies and even be reincarnated.

The self and its components in the Norse religion differ from the concept of the soul in Christianity, which is considered a unique part of the self. It never detaches itself from the person except in death. In fact, the word soul or "sal" in the Norse language didn't exist in the ancient religion and only came into being after the arrival of Christianity.

Understanding the self and its components will give you a better idea of how the Norse people comprehended the idea of the soul.

The Hamr

The word *"hamr"* is pronounced like "hammer," meaning skin or shape. It represents the person's physical appearance, and it is the visible and solid part of the self. The body has always been understood as a fixed aspect that can never be altered. However, in the Norse religion, the physical form can be changed. Your hamr can change after death, or the mind can manipulate it. Some people can also alter their physical appearance by performing certain spells. Norse mythology mentions warriors who would transform into wolves or bears.

The word *"hamr"* was used in the context of describing shapeshifting. For instance, *"hamhleypa"* is the Norse word for a shapeshifter, and skipta hömum (hömum is the noun of hamr) translates to "shifting one's shape." The hamr doesn't accompany the person to the afterlife.

The Hugr

The word "*hugr*" means the thought or mind, and it is the first invisible part of the self. It can also refer to your will, emotions, consciousness, and personality and is closely associated with the concept of the inner self. It represents your desires, intuition, thoughts, and presence. Your hugr represents how you make people feel in your company.

Some people possess strong hugrs and can use this ability to impact others from a distance using just their thoughts. Sometimes, your hugr could leave your body and enter another person's. For instance, if you envy someone and think negatively of them, you can make them ill. Your hugr or thoughts travel to the person you are thinking about and impact their health and body. A person can do this subconsciously without intending to harm anyone.

The hugr doesn't remain in the body after death and usually accompanies the soul to the afterlife.

The Fylgja

Look at any ancient illustration of witches. You'll usually find them with animal or bird companions like ravens or cats. This type of spirit is referred to as fylgjur (plural of Fylgja), a Norse word pronounced as "Filg-yur." Fylgja, pronounced "Filg-ya," means pursue, guide, lead, follow, belong to, to side with, or help, and its noun means an "attendant spirit."

These spirits usually take the form of an animal; in some rare cases, they can be human. However, not everyone can see them. You must have specific abilities like the gift of second sight. One can also see these spirits in dreams or while dying, even without any special abilities

The moment before someone dies, they can see their dead fylgja. This indicates that you and your fylgja are connected; when you get sick, it gets sick, and when you die, it dies, and vice versa. Although the fylgja can be separated from the self, it shares the same fate as its owner.

The fylgja shares many other aspects with its owner. For instance, a gluttonous person can have a pig fylgja, a violent person can have a wolf fylgja, a shy person can have a deer fylgja, and a noble person can have a bear fylgja.

Although the fylgja should follow its owner, many stories have mentioned how it reaches the intended destination before the person. Your fylgja can also see and hear things that you can't and uses this ability to protect you from harm.

The Hamingja

The last aspect of the self is the *hamingja*, pronounced: "hahm-ing-ya." It represents a person's luck, but in Norse mythology, the concept of luck is different. It is considered a characteristic like intelligence or strength inherited from your family, and it greatly impacts your life and future. For instance, it can make you wealthy or successful, and it can also act as a protective spirit.

Although it is a part of the self, it is considered a separate entity that can sometimes separate itself from the person. For instance, when a person dies, their hamingja doesn't remain with them in the afterlife. It can be reincarnated in one of the person's descendants, especially if they are named after its owner. Norse literature also tells stories of a hamingja choosing a family member and attaching itself to them. On other occasions, a person can choose before or after dying who can take their hamingja. You could also lend your hamingja to others if they are suffering from bad fortune and want to change their luck.

The hamingja usually takes the form of a huge, strong woman resembling the Valkyrie.

Meditation Technique

Meditating requires you to dig deep within and transcend your physical form to eliminate the boundaries between you and your soul.

Instructions:
1. Find a quiet, peaceful place with no distractions.
2. Set a timer for 15 minutes.
3. Sit on the floor with your legs crossed and your hands on your lap, like the lotus position that many people take when doing yoga. If it makes you uncomfortable, choose another position, but you should be on the floor, not on a chair, sofa, or bed.
4. Close your eyes and take a few deep breaths to clear your mind. You can play binaural beats to help you relax.
5. Only focus on the sound of the beats, and don't let your mind wander off or your thoughts distract you.
6. Focus on your inner self and shift your awareness from your body and the world around you to your soul.

7. Remain focused on every beat. If distractions or thoughts creep in, quickly return your focus to the binaural beats. Keep doing that until you are completely relaxed, and your mind is quiet.
8. You should now be completely unaware of time and space. You are now at one with the self and connected to it on a higher level.
9. Remain in this state until the 15 minutes are up, then slowly open your eyes.

Norse religion is unique and stands out from other beliefs. Unlike many ancient mythologies, their deities have no power over where the soul ends up in the afterlife. Their view of the soul is also different, consisting of various components that can each be a separate entity. Although many ancient cultures at the time believed in judgment and gave their deities power over how and where they spent the afterlife, the Norse had a different perception. As a result, to this day, it remains one of the most fascinating religions in the world.

Chapter 5: Fylgja: Finding Your Guardian

In a land long ago, a young man eagerly awaited the grand party of the year. Each day, he counted down the hours and anticipated the festivities to come. Little did he know, however, that a wicked witch was plotting his demise on that very night.

Thankfully, the man's fylgja was aware of the danger. It tried to warn him through vivid dreams for five nights, but he remained oblivious to its messages. As the event approached, he remained clueless about the signs his fylgja was sending him.

With time running out, the fylgja took matters into its own hands. It made the young man ill, preventing him from attending the party and unknowingly saving his life.

Such is the power of the fylgja - a guardian spirit that will go to any length to protect those under its care. Sadly, many remain unaware of their existence and miss the daily messages they send. Discovering and bonding with your fylgja, however, can transform your life in ways beyond your imagination.

Discovering and bonding with your fylgja can profoundly impact your life, but the journey to connect with your guardian spirit can be challenging. Thankfully, this chapter offers practical techniques to help you establish a relationship with your spirit guide.

Meditation can help you connect with your fylgja.[15]

Through meditation, visualization, and other methods, you can learn to recognize and communicate with your fylgja. By honing your intuition and opening yourself up to the messages it sends, you can tap into the wisdom and guidance of your guardian spirit.

Whether you seek protection, clarity, or simply a deeper connection with the spiritual realm, the techniques presented in this chapter can help you forge a bond with your fylgja and unlock its full potential.

Meditation Technique

Tools:

- White sage
- Pen and paper

Instructions:

1. Before you begin, set the intention that you are performing this meditation technique to connect with your spirit guide. You can say something like, *"I am taking a journey to the spirit world to connect with my guardian."*

2. Prepare a sacred space for meditation. Cleanse it by burning white sage and letting the smoke purify it.

3. Move around the room and call on the four directions (north, south, east, and west).

4. Then, honor the four elements, Earth, Water, Air, and Fire, and honor the Spirit as well.
5. Say, *"I call on the Earth's energy to keep me grounded while I head to the invisible realms and connect with my spirit guide."*
6. *"I call on the Water's energy, praying that its currents flow easily and open the pathway that will take me to my spirit guide."*
7. *"I call on the Air's energy to bring the light and bestow upon me the gift of clarity so I can trust my intuition while I journey to meet my spirit guide."*
8. *"I call on the Fire's energy to illuminate my path in the invisible realms while I connect with my spirit guide."*
9. *"I call on the Spirit's energy, Grandmother Moon, Grandfather Sun, my dear ancestors, and all other helpful spirits who can hear me. Protect me and keep me safe while I head to the invisible realms and connect with my spirit guide."*
10. Write on the piece of paper all the questions you want to ask your spirit guide.
11. Now, prepare yourself for meditation.
12. Sit in the sacred space in the lotus position.
13. Breathe in and out slowly and deeply for one or two minutes, and feel your body relax with every breath.
14. Clear your mind and only focus on the present moment.
15. Repeat your intention again under your breath.
16. Close your eyes and visualize yourself standing in the middle of a big forest with beautiful scenery all around you. Take in your surroundings.
17. Wherever you look, you see colorful flowers and tall green trees.
18. A pathway in front of you will take you to your spirit guide.
19. You walk towards it.
20. You feel the air in your hair and the warm sunlight on your skin.
21. While walking on the pathway, you feel a sense of tranquility washing over you. You feel joyful because you know who is waiting for you on the other side.

22. You see the wind blowing through the trees, and you see that you are almost there.
23. You feel the protection of the four elements.
24. You can't wait to finally meet your guardian and have all your questions answered.
25. You have finally arrived at your destination and see a big ball of white light.
26. You walk closer and step into it.
27. Now, you are standing before your spirit guide.
28. Look closer to see the figure standing in front of you. It could be a bird, an animal, or a ball of energy. Whatever appears in front of you is your guardian.
29. Ask, *"Are you my spirit guide?"* and wait for an answer.
30. Ask, *"What's your name?"*
31. Whatever name they give you, use it to address them.
32. Now, your spirit guide will tell you,

    "From the day you were born, I have been by your side. You are never on your own; I am always with you, guiding, helping, and protecting you."
33. You are overwhelmed by emotions knowing that you aren't alone and feel connected to them.
34. You walk toward them and hug them.
35. Now, you will ask them all the questions you have prepared before the meditation. Don't hold back, and ask anything that comes to mind. Your spirit guide is there to help you and will do everything in its power to give you the answers you seek.
36. After you have finished asking your questions, tell them that you are leaving but that you'll meet again. Your spirit guide will tell you, "Even though you can't always see me, I am constantly walking beside you. Whenever you need me, just call out to me."
37. Give them another hug and express your gratitude for all their help.
38. Return to the same road by exiting through the ball of light and walking back on the same pathway.

39. You feel content and at peace after this spiritual experience and the knowledge that your spirit guide will always keep you safe.
40. When you are ready to exit the meditation, take a few deep breaths, then open your eyes.
41. Be on the lookout for signs because your spirit guide will send you messages through songs, animals, symbols, etc., so keep your eyes and ears open.

Focus on Your Dreams

Pay attention to everything you see in your dreams because your guardian can either reveal itself to you or send you messages in the dream world.

Instructions:
1. When you lie in bed before you drift to sleep, ask your guardian to reveal him/herself to you in your dream. You can say, "Guardian who always looks out for me and serves my best interest, please visit me in my dreams tonight. I am prepared to receive your wisdom and grateful for your constant guidance and support. I promise to remember my dream when I wake up in the morning."
2. Keep repeating the intention until you fall asleep. Leave a notebook and pen by your side so you can write down your dream as soon as you wake up.
3. The next morning, write down everything you remember, even the details you think are irrelevant or unimportant.
4. After you have finished, read everything you wrote and analyze all the signs and symbols to figure out who your spirit guide is and what it is trying to communicate to you.

Scrying

Scrying, also called crystal gazing, is a divination practice that originated in ancient Persia. It involves staring at a crystal ball, mirror, water, or any reflective surface to receive the answers you seek.

Tools:
- A bowl of water (preferably a dark bowl since it will make it easy for you to concentrate)

- Table
- A crystal (preferably crystal quartz)
- Matches or a lighter
- 2 candles
- White sage

Instructions:
1. Choose a place for scrying. You can do it indoors or outdoors, but it has to be dark. If you practice indoors, turn off the light and shut the curtains. If you practice outdoors, do it at night.
2. Place the bowl of water on the table, then drop the crystal in it.
3. Cleanse your space using white sage.
4. Light the candles, then place them on either side of the bowl. The flames should reflect on the water's surface.
5. Enter into a trance state by meditating while focusing on your breathing and listening to soft music.
6. Begin scrying when you feel focused, relaxed, and at peace.
7. Sit comfortably, gaze into the bowl of water, and relax your eyes.
8. Focus on the crystal to prevent your eyes from wandering off.
9. Remain calm and be patient. Scrying isn't easy and can take a while to master.
10. Repeat the intention of finding your spirit guide to yourself.
11. Keep your eyes and face relaxed.
12. Take deep breaths from your stomach.
13. You'll begin to see images coming and going, don't hold on to them, as this will only make the process harder. Allow them and the emotions that accompany them to come and go freely.
14. It is normal for your mind to wander off, don't force it to come back. Just make sure that your eyes are focused on the water bowl.
15. You can start seeing an image, word, or scene playing out.
16. When you have finished, contemplate what you saw for a few minutes.

17. You may not find your spirit or animal guide right away. Scrying takes time and practice, so do it as often as possible until you find your guardian.
18. You can use any other reflective image like fire, oil, wax, clouds, smoke, crystal, or look into someone's eye. Choose the method you feel drawn to the most.

Animal Oracle Cards

Using animal oracle cards is a quick and sure way to find your guardian animal.

Instructions:

1. Connect with the cards by carrying them around wherever you go for a few days, or play with them at every chance you get. Introduce them to your energy by constantly touching and using them. This will make working with them easier and give you accurate results.
2. Set the intention of what you hope the cards reveal to you. You can say, *"I want the cards to reveal my guardian animal to me."*
3. Take a few deep and slow breaths and focus on the present moment and your intention.
4. Shuffle the deck seven times or more until you feel your energy has merged with the cards' energy.
5. Spread the cards face down, and place your hands over them.
6. Once you feel pulled to a card, pick it up. This is the card that will reveal to you your guardian animal.
7. Look at the card to identify your guardian animal.
8. Sit with it for a few minutes to try to connect with the card and get acquainted with your spirit animal.
9. Write down in your journal how the card makes you feel.

You can also meditate on the card.

Instructions:

1. Sit comfortably in a quiet room with no distractions.
2. Hold the card in your hand.
3. Close your eyes and take a few deep breaths.
4. Feel your body relax with every breath you take.

5. Clear your mind and be present in the moment.
6. Visualize the card and get lost in your imagination.
7. Observe all the details you see in the visualization. Notice all the symbols you see since your guardian animal can send you messages through your meditation.
8. Try to understand the message they are trying to send to you.
9. After you have finished, express your gratitude for what you received from your spirit guide.
10. Take a few deep breaths, then slowly open your eyes.

Bibliomancy

Bibliomancy is another ancient divination technique that involves finding the answers you seek in a book that calls to you. It is one of the oldest divination methods, and many people still use it to find their spirit guide.

Instructions:
1. Stand in front of your book collection. If you don't have one, go to a bookstore or your local library.
2. Close your eyes and set an intention that you want to find your spirit guide in one of these books.
3. Move your hands over the books and let your intuition guide you; the book will call to you.
4. Once you feel the urge to pick up a book, do it.
5. Open your eyes and randomly open the book and take a quick look. You can find a word or a picture that reveals your guardian to you.
6. You can also wait a few minutes before opening the book for a page number to come to you, then open it and read it.
7. Bibliomancy may not work the first time you try it, especially if you aren't connected to your intuition. Keep practicing until you feel like a book is pulling you in.
8. Sometimes, your spirit guide will not give you a clear sign and just send you a clue. Use it and keep searching and exploring until you figure it out.

Vision Quest

Instructions:
1. After you wake up in the morning, perform a simple meditation.
2. Sit in a comfortable position in a quiet room.
3. Close your eyes and take a few deep breaths.
4. Ask your spirit animal to show themselves to you by sending signs or clues.
5. Keep your eyes open for messages throughout the day. Your guardian animal can show you symbols that reveal their identity to you or just give you hints. For instance, if it is a bird, you can see feathers everywhere you go or hear birds chirping.
6. Your guardian animal can also directly show you who they are. For instance, if it is a wolf, you'll see images or videos of wolves everywhere online, in books, on street art, or a friend will randomly mention the animal to you or buy you a pendant in the shape of a wolf.
7. Do this meditation every morning. At night, write down all the signs you saw during the day.
8. If you see more than one animal, focus on the one you see the most.
9. Remember, when your guardian animal decides to reveal itself to you, it will keep sending you messages and signs until you finally take notice.

Nature

Your spirit guide is most likely an animal or a bird, so it will use natural elements to reveal itself to you. Even when you discover your fylgia, you can use nature whenever you want to connect with it or ask a question.

Instructions:
1. Find a place in nature like a lake, stream, or park.
2. Stare at the trees, flowers, water, clouds, moon, etc., and try to see a face.
3. If you see the face of an animal that has been appearing to you a lot lately, it could be your animal guide.

Repeated Signs

The universe usually sends you messages through repetitive signs like symbols, names, or numbers. Your spirit guides can also send messages or reveal themselves to you by repeating the same sign repeatedly until you notice.

Instructions:
1. Set a clear intention either out loud or internally, or say a prayer like

    "Dear (mention the name of the Norse deity of your choice or call on the spirits of your ancestors), I implore you to help me find my spirit guide. Please, send me signals, signs, or symbols every day. Thank you."
2. Keep your eyes open every day for repetitive and unusual objects, places, symbols, names, or numbers that appear to you.
3. Write them down and after a week, reflect on them and try to decipher their meaning.

Release Your Worries to Your Spirit Guide

If you are struggling to make a decision or looking for a solution to a problem, release your worries to your spirit guide.

Instructions:
1. Sit in a quiet space and clear your thoughts.
2. Repeat this mantra *"I am releasing (name the issue) to my spirit guide so they can help me find a solution."*
3. Be on the lookout for messages or signs they will send you to help you with your problem.

Sometimes, you can try everything, but your fylgia won't reveal itself to you. This doesn't mean that it is refusing to connect with you. It just wants you to keep searching because there is a lesson for you on this journey. Don't give up. Eventually, you'll find your fylgia. In other cases, its messages or symbols can be so clear and loud that it will be impossible to miss them. Keep your eyes open.

Once you find your guardian, seek their help and guidance whenever you face a problem. Understand their messages and warnings because they can save your life. Constantly express your gratitude to them to show your appreciation for all their help.

Chapter 6: The Magic of Seidr

Seidr is a common spiritual and shamanic practice in Norse Paganism and is mainly concerned with fate. It was used to uncover the nuances of fate and, if necessary, subtly change them however the practitioner wanted. According to ancient lore, the practice was used for both good and evil purposes. While practitioners of Seidr were notorious for casting curses on people, they also cast protective spells and provided charms for empowerment and spiritual protection.

Seidr was mainly practiced by women.[16]

Traditionally associated with the goddess Freyja, Seidr was mainly practiced by women. These women were highly respected members of their communities, unlike male practitioners, who were often ridiculed and labeled effeminate. The mystery associated with Seidr was a feminine trait in Norse traditions and culture. Because of this, men who practiced Seidr were thought to be breaking gender norms. Even the mighty god Odin (believed to be the most skillful Seidr practitioner amongst the deities) was mocked for using what was considered feminine powers. However, many male practitioners idolized him due to his other masculine characteristics.

This chapter will explore the concepts of Seidr and the Völva and help you to understand the different levels of trance a shaman can reach. Then, you'll find a step-by-step guide to going on a safe Seidr journey.

Before You Start

It is necessary to emphasize that Norse Shamanism, or any other shamanic practice, is safer for beginners when practiced with an experienced guide. If you're a solitary practitioner, you should gain experience in trance and journeying methods before proceeding to higher levels. Shamanic practices can harm your mental well-being if you aren't adequately prepared or have psychological issues. When you enter into a trance, you'll receive messages in the form of auditory or visual signs. This can be overwhelming even if you don't have mental health issues. It may take some time to get used to the messages and learn how to decipher them. If you feel overwhelmed or have symptoms like severe anxiety and hallucinations during or after your practice, you should stop and seek help from a mental health professional. Similarly, if you're already struggling with mental health issues, don't start practicing Seidr (or any other form of shamanism) until you've addressed them.

What Is Shamanism?

Shamanism is a spiritual practice that involves gaining knowledge or powers through a trance-like state. The abilities you could obtain in this state include divination, healing, or guidance for the living or dead.

The term "shamanism" originates from the Manchu-Tungus word saman and can be translated to *"the one who knows."* Historical records suggest that it was widespread among ancient tribes in Africa, the Arctic, Australia, Asia, and America. Shamanism was typically practiced by hunting and gathering communities.

While it's unclear when the ancient Germanic tribes adopted shamanism into their practices, myths suggest they weren't strangers to it. Odin, the king of the Germanic gods, was a well-known shaman, and he practiced Seidr after he learned from the goddess Freyja. Some sources suggest that Odin's name can be translated as *"the master of inspiration"* or *"the master of ecstasy."* His shamanic journeys are documented in several myths, sagas, and poems, including a famous Eddic poem named "Baldur's Dreams." It describes Odin traveling to the underworld after the death of his son Baldur. He used the trance to ride Sleipnir, his eight-legged horse, and cross the divide between the realms. There, he asked a dead seeress for advice on how to revive Baldur.

Odin's two ravens, Hugin and Munin, are believed to have been familiar spirit companions, which is typical for those practicing shamanism. A shaman must die and be reborn to gain the power of entering a trance - which Odin did during his trial at the Tree of Life.

According to legend, Odin ignited battles among tribes to collect the fiercest warriors' souls. Some of the warriors he selected were also suggested to have the ability to practice Seidr or another form of shamanism. According to the Ynglinga Saga, some of Odin's warriors went into battle as if in a trance. They acted like animals and didn't wear any armor. They couldn't be harmed, and they constantly won battles. This indicates that they became possessed by the spirits of animals. Other sources describe these warriors shifting their shapes to become wolves and bears.

What Is Seidr?

Seidr is an ancient form of Norse shamanism. Besides trances, it also relies on magic to foretell fate, identify one's purpose in life, and manipulate fate to create desired changes. Practitioners did all of this by using trances and magic to symbolically weave the threads of fate in a way that they attract desired situations and events. Their rituals and ceremonies typically began with them entering a trance where they would communicate with the spirit world and harness its wisdom. Their purposes included casting curses or blessings, bringing empowerment and protection, or a prophecy about future events.

Seidr rituals were also used for clairvoyance, an approach that allowed the practitioner to locate hidden objects or thoughts. It was also used to attract abundance and good luck, ensure a good harvest, and hunt by controlling the weather and conjuring animals. When used for malicious purposes, Seidr was used to induce sickness, make a land barren, or prevent an enemy from winning in battle. Instead of curses, the practitioner could also tell people false prophecies to lead them toward the wrong path. Due to these false readings, practitioners could make people injure and kill their adversaries, whether in a battle or in a simple disagreement. Those who mastered the art of weaving or changing fate were known as the Norns. They were said to be the first and most proficient practitioners.

The god Odin and the goddess Freya are two significant Vanir and Aesir deities who mastered the art of Seidr. As the divine archetypes of male and female practitioners, their duality plays a unique role in a gendered practice like Seidr.

What Is a Völva?

The goddess Freyja was thought to serve as a role model for Völva - a female practitioner of Seidr. According to Norse lore, Freyja was the first deity to bring the practice of Seidr to the realm of the gods. Due to their healing powers and ability to perform magic and provide spiritual guidance, a Völva was a highly respected member of their community. Being a leading figure herself, a Völva was usually respected and protected by their clan or tribe's leaders. Male Seidr practitioners were called seers, but they were much rarer.

A Völva roamed the towns and performed magic in return for several forms of compensation, including room and board. Many sagas and heroic poems (most notably: The Saga of Erik the Red, and The Insight of the Völva, respectively) offer detailed descriptions of a Völva and her practices.

Even though they were treated with respect, Völvas were often segregated from society. This had both negative and positive connotations. On one hand, a Völva was feared and often stigmatized because they could cast powerful curses. They also led nomadic lifestyles, which set them apart from others. Yet, they were also sought-after and esteemed because people knew how much they could help the community. The figure of a Völva is often compared to the Veleda, the Germanic prophetess who was very respected among her tribe.

While there is little evidence of Seidr being widely practiced among men, it was considered an inappropriate activity for men in the Viking era.

They had rigid gender norms, with men being associated with male roles like hunting and fighting in battles. This made it shameful for a man to adopt some aspects of female practices. Men who practiced this art were labeled unmanly (the common term was *ergi*), a great insult at the time.

One of the most notable reasons for ostracizing male Seidr practitioners was the weaving aspect of the practice, something only women were allowed to do. Despite this, some men still engaged in Seidr and even regarded it as their occupation.

The Tools of Seidr

One of the most indispensable tools of Seidr was the shamanic staff. While there is little evidence of its function, it is believed that the Sidr staff allowed the practitioner to focus on their intent. It also had a grounding effect because when set on the ground, it provided a connection to nature. It could attract nature's power and concentrate it. The staff could also act as a transportation tool when the practice included a journey.

Seidr practitioners often use herbs.[17]

Other tools employed by Völvas and other Seidr practitioners were charms and herbs - which acted as protective agents during the practice. Shamanic work often involves connecting with spirits, but not all are helpful or well-intentioned. Charms could also be used for divination, along with runes. The Völvas were often depicted wearing a blue cloak, which they used to guide the souls of the departed to Hel. Freyja herself collected some of the souls, and the Völvas had the same abilities.

Different Levels of Consciousness

There are many ways to enter trance states, or "altered states of consciousness." Shamans and indigenous groups across nations believed this state was a bridge between the subconscious and spiritual realms. Being in this state enables the practitioner to connect more effectively with spirits and divine beings. Besides gathering wisdom and knowledge to use in life, it also helps them heighten their spirituality.

When you enter a trance state, you are neither asleep nor awake. Being in an altered state of consciousness requires you to travel through different levels of consciousness.

The 5 levels of Consciousness:

Level 1: Very Light Trance - It requires you to become more aware of your thoughts, feelings, and physical sensations. Practicing mindful meditation is a great way to reach this state.

Level 2: Light Trance - This is a dream-like level of consciousness that every person experiences without realizing it. For example, when you find yourself lost in thought while watching a movie, reading a book, or completely forgetting what you're doing, you're entering this state.

Level 3: Medium Trance - Also known as the "flow" state, the third level of consciousness is a little deeper than the previous one. In this state of consciousness, you lose awareness of the time, surroundings, and bodily sensations.

Level 4: Deep Trance - Most people enter into this state when asleep or falling into hypnagogia - a rapid and somewhat confusing state of consciousness that happens right before you drift off. It's caused by your conscious mind switching off and giving control to the subconscious. This level of consciousness is characterized by peculiar mental images and sometimes even hallucinations.

Level 5: Very Deep Trance - You completely lose consciousness during this stage, and it's described as being a deep, dreamless sleep. During Seidr, the most effective spiritual states are unlocked during the light, medium, or deep trance states.

A Seidr Cleansing Ritual

This simple cleansing ritual can be easily incorporated into your preparation routine for a shamanic journey. It uses juniper wood (you can substitute it for any other sacred pagan wood or herb). In ancient times, juniper was used for shamanic practices, cleansing, invoking spirits, or ancestral communication. The goal is to purify yourself from negative influences and have a successful journey. Besides cleansing yourself, you can also use this ritual to purge your home of toxic energies.

Instructions:

1. Gather your wood or herbs and tie them into a bunch to create a smudge stick. Alternatively, you can buy a premade one. Open your windows so the negativity can leave your presence as soon as possible.
2. Do a quick grounding meditation exercise using your preferred method. This can be listening to drumming music, repeating a mantra, breathwork, or anything else that helps you focus.
3. Light your smudging stick at one end and wait until it starts smoking.
4. Start moving the stick around whatever item, space, or person you want to cleanse. If it's you, envelope yourself in a smoke cloud. If it's your space, walk around in a clockwise direction, carrying the stick with you. Stop and linger at the corners, as negativity tends to collect in these spaces.
5. If you're using any tools before, during, or after the Seidr ritual, cleanse them by fanning smoke over them.
6. When you've finished, dip the stick into sand to extinguish it. Don't blow on it or use water, as this could offend the spirit you're trying to connect to.

A Safe Seidr Journeying Exercise

Before you start your journey, you must have an open mind, a clear intention, a quiet place to work, and a picture in your head of an entry point to another world. Additional tools like a blindfold, music, audio of drumming, and a stick (to act as a staff) may also come in handy.

Instructions:

1. Find a quiet space where you won't be disturbed. If you're inside, turn off your electronics and ask whoever is around to leave you alone.
2. Lie or sit down and relax your body and mind. Use the floor and not your bed. Otherwise, you may fall asleep instead of

entering a trance.

3. Take a few deep breaths, holding each at the end of the inhale for 3 seconds. After, exhale until you've pushed all the air out of your lungs. Ideally, each inhale-exhale cycle should last longer than the previous one. Use your diaphragm to deepen your breath and make it last longer.

4. If you're using one, put on a blindfold. If you're uncomfortable using a blindfold, you can work in a dark room and simply close your eyes.

5. State your intention after relaxing your mind and chasing away all unrelated ideas. Make sure it sends a clear signal of what you want to achieve on this journey. At the same time, it should sound more like a respectful appeal than a goal you want to obtain at all costs.

6. Put on the music or drumming, and start focusing on it. As you do, visualize the entry point to the desired world and loudly reiterate your intention a couple of times.

7. Once you have the entrance in front of you, cross it. Be prepared to pay attention to your surroundings by using all your senses. You may see, hear, smell, or feel things. Don't be afraid to explore whatever channels have opened up to you; they could hold messages you want to explore further.

8. If you experience something negative, you can choose not to pay attention to it. If you can, retrace your steps or open your eyes to leave that world. The rest of the journey depends on your intention and purpose. For example, if you want to connect with an ancestral spirit or animal spirit guide, look for the signs of them reaching out to you.

9. If you're unsure whether you've encountered the right spirit, ask them. Or, look for four similar signs. If you meet four similar signs, it's a good indicator that a spirit is communicating with you.

10. You can spend as much time on your journey as you like. However, the process can be somewhat overwhelming. Because of this, beginners should start with an 8-10 minute journey. Later on, as you become more confident in your practice, you can increase the time.

11. If you're using a shamanic drumming tape as a basis for your trance, choose the ones that signal the time to end the journey. If you're using music, select the one that lasts as long as you want the journey to last. Or, you can set a timer to signal when you should end your travels. Use a subtle alarm sound to avoid getting jarred out of your journey.
12. To come back, retrace your steps to the entry point. Walk slowly, memorizing your path in case you want to return in the future. This way, you'll be able to travel to and from that world with greater ease and efficiency.
13. When you've returned, stay still for a moment, and don't open your eyes yet. Reflect on your journey for a moment and stay grounded. Pay attention to how you feel - in your mind, body, and spirit. Does anything feel different than before your journey?
14. Reflect on the experiences you had and the messages you've received. Were you able to decipher them? Did you identify where they came from and what they mean? If not, you can write them down and revisit them later on. Sometimes, the messages only become apparent after some reflection.

Chapter 7: Utesitta: Sitting Out, Seeking Within

Utesitta translates to "sitting out" and is a form of meditation for anyone seeking stillness and answers to pressing questions by connecting with the Spirit. It involves sitting out in a natural environment, entering into a light trance, and performing acts of magic. In this chapter, you'll discover the origin of the Utesitta ritual and learn how it was used by the Völvas in ancient times. You'll also learn about the importance of breathwork and concentration for this ritual. Last but not least, you'll receive handy instructions on performing the Utesitta meditation and the breathwork that will allow you to focus during the ritual.

What Is the Utesitta Ritual, and What Are Its Origins?

Utesitta is an ancient meditation ritual commonly practiced by the Völva and other shamanic practitioners of the Norse religion. While there is very little information on the exact origins of this practice, it's believed that its roots lie in Germanic pagan traditions. The way Utesitta was practiced by the Norse shamans seems to support this belief. According to the lore, the Völva would venture into the burial mounds of the dead ancestors, sit on top of them, and meditate until they summoned the ancestor's spirit and obtained their wisdom. The Völva were powerful shamans and practitioners of magic, and they often ventured into divination as well. However, it's believed that most of the knowledge obtained by the Völva came from ancestral spirits. In essence, they used the Utesitta in the same way as they used runic divination. Whether they wanted to learn the outcome of a battle, decide whether to attack, retreat, surrender, or know whether the year's harvest would be successful, the Völva could consult the ancestors and obtain the answers.

In Uppsala, Sweden, archaeologists found burial mounds with a flat top, which suggests that they were built with the Utesitta ritual in mind. The work of the Völva was clearly visible from the bottom, and they could work comfortably. The Utesitta ritual often required a lot of time and focus, which was physically and mentally demanding for the practitioner. Sometimes, Völvas would receive requests from several people, who all sought answers about their futures. Sitting up on the burial ground, the Völva meditated until they found the answers that were hidden from others.

The Poetic Edda also references Utesitta in a poem about the hero Svipdagsmal. In need of some spiritual empowerment, Svipdagsmal sat on the burial mound of his mother. He meditated until he was able to rouse his mother's soul. She gave him advice and nine magical charms that would later help him on his quests.

Another example of Utesitta being referenced in the Poetic Edda comes from the poem of Voluspa. In it, a Völva is described using Utisetta to obtain a prophecy, which she delivered to the children of Heimdall. This particular foretelling included all the events that would happen in the world, including Ragnarok.

The Importance of Breathwork and Concentration

Utesitta is quite lengthy, which makes it rather challenging to maintain concentration. The longer you're sitting or standing focusing on your intention, the harder it is for your brain to exclude incoming thoughts. The same applies to the body - the longer you spend in one position, the more likely it will distract you by signaling you to move. This is when acquiring adequate breathwork comes in handy.

Moreover, Utesitta is not only about clearing your mind. It's about entering a state of altered consciousness - similar to a trance. In this state, you can connect to the other realms and speak with the deities, your ancestors, and spiritual guides. Breathwork can also help you remain focused on your intention of communicating with the beings from other realms and deciphering their messages, regardless of how long the journey takes.

The idea of breathwork is also tied to Odin. As one of the three brothers (half gods and half-giants) who created the world and people, Odin had an undeniable role in tying everything to the natural world. He was the one who breathed life into the three trunks the first humans were created from. It is believed that the Völva and other Norse shamans could connect to this life-giving divine essence through breathwork. Even nowadays, practitioners equate focusing on one breath with the idea of Odin giving life -and use it to empower themselves through Odin. They use this power to stay focused during Utesitta and harness the answers they seek.

Breathwork is a process of controlled and conscious breathing used to awaken your inner self. When you have control over your breathing, you can explore the subconscious part of your mind. It's a journey that takes you back to your core self. You can reach places beyond the realm of your intellect and awaken ancient memories - which promotes better spiritual communication during Utesitta. You can use your breath to awaken your spiritual potential, creativity, memory, and willpower for advanced visualization and communication. Through your breath, you can communicate with every part of your body to align it with nature's power and use everything around you to gain the wisdom you seek. Breathwork can also help you heal traumas and resolve emotions that could interfere with spiritual communication or hinder your ability to focus during your work.

How Does Utesitta Differ from Journeying?

The main difference between Utesitta mediation and shamanic journeying is the length of the practice. Seidr and other forms of shamanic journeying typically don't last longer than 15-20 minutes. For an experienced shamanic practitioner, 15 minutes is more than enough time to seek the required information. For beginners, it's also enough time to practice, even if they don't get answers immediately. Utesitta, on the other hand, is a much longer exercise. It can take hours or even days to complete depending on your experience level and the answers you seek.

Another notable difference is that shamans typically enter a trance-like state while journeying, whereas with Utesitta, you must stay right at the edge of entering this state to remain conscious enough to communicate with the spirit you're trying to connect with. Not only that, but you enter this state through a guided path. For example, you can listen to drumming and enter a trance to heal trauma or learn something from your ancestors. Or, you can journey to the spirit world and meet the spirits there.

The states of consciousness in Norse shamanism look like this:

- **Very light trance** - Achieved through mediation and simple breathwork
- **Light trance** - Used in Utesitta
- **Deep trance** - Achieved through shamanic journeying
- **Very deep trance** - Reached through guided shamanic traveling or magic

Utesitta Meditation in Modern Times

Nowadays, Utesitta is viewed as a spiritual embodiment of an experience of one's self as part of the natural world. There are many ways modern practitioners experience themselves as part of nature. One of these is finding a sitting spot where they won't be disturbed when practicing deep meditation. You can start with a simple 15-minute meditation to slow your breathing and calm your mind. Listening to natural sounds around you can help you with this. Feel free to return to this spot and do longer meditations. The more attuned you become to the place, the easier it will be to focus for longer periods in one sitting. Experienced practitioners perform Utesitta through the entire night - from sundown to daybreak.

Utesitta involves sitting still in nature.[18]

Here is a testimony from a modern-day Utesitta practitioner:

"My journey began just before sunset, as the sun was dipping below the horizon. The night was quiet and cold, and the sky was cloudy. I sat in a quiet place, away from everyone else, wrapped in my cloak. After deepening my breath, I started traveling through the landscape and only stopped when I reached an ancient oak tree and the well beside it. I touched the charm that I wore around my neck. I let myself fall down into the well. While traveling downward, I was aware of the oak tree above me, but time slowly dissolved. I felt compelled to take a deep breath, and when I released it, I was standing on the ground, having resurfaced from the well. The sky was much darker, and I saw four crows flying eastward. Since my purpose was to reach out to the goddess Freyja, I started praying to her. I saw a picture of someone laying a wooden bowl under the oak tree, pouring mead into the bowl, and stirring it clockwise three times. They offered the mead to the goddess, asking for a good harvest in return. I read the runes etched into the wooden bowl and heard people chanting a beautiful song dedicated to Freyja. Focusing on this song helped me steady my breath and focus on my intention. After some time, I felt the answer form. I saw myself standing in Freyjas's hall, feeling the pull to enter. I felt welcomed as I watched the candles burn. I knew I was between realms, and my answer was suddenly in my head. It felt complete, and I expressed my gratitude. I closed my eyes, and when I opened them, I was once again among the modern world, sitting in my secluded spot while the sun was about to rise." Chiara

Beginners are advised to perform Utesitta by following an experienced guide. Remember, this incredibly demanding exercise requires plenty of focus and willpower. Establishing contact with someone from another world can also be overwhelming, so you should always be extra careful about how you go about doing it. A guide can help you reach the desired state of consciousness safely and efficiently, so you can obtain the wisdom you seek.

Even with a guide by your side, you can't expect to dive into Utesitta immediately. Before attempting it, you should master effective breathwork and meditation techniques, which will train your mind to focus for longer periods of time and your body to stay relaxed for as long as required. After becoming confident in meditation and breathwork, you can move on to attempting to enter into a light trance. Practice this, as well, to get comfortable working in this state and see how you can use your natural powers while in a trance. Once you are comfortable entering this light trance, you can move on to doing an Utesitta meditation.

Nowadays, this in-depth meditation can also be performed for similar purposes as it was used by the Norse people in ancient times. You can use it to gain answers about future events from ancestors and spiritual guides or ask them for their insight about a particular situation. Sitting outside lets you reform your much-needed connection to nature and receive inspiration or guidance. Some practitioners use Utesitta as a channeling practice - to harness the energies of nature and the universe.

Many practitioners find covering themselves with a cloak or a shawl useful to block out visual distractions. Once the person resets their senses and blocks out distractions, they typically remove the fabric and look upon the world with new eyes. Their other senses will be heightened, which helps them enter a trance-like state.

Utesitta Exercises

Here is a beginner-friendly way to perform Utesitta mediation. It's designed to be done overnight, not just for a couple of hours. However, if you are uncomfortable doing it all night, feel free to reduce the time. As you're sitting in one place as a beginner, you'll probably feel compelled to ask yourself whether the exercise has a purpose. This is normal, but it just means you must train yourself to be more patient. It is something that happens to all practitioners. Everyone needs to go through that before they can understand the true spiritual meaning of the practice.

Preparatory Tips

Utsitta is traditionally performed on a mound or a faery hill. However, suppose you don't have mounds around. In that case, your ancestors' graves will work, too - especially if you want to communicate with their spirits. Before you embark on your meditation journey, think about your purpose. Establishing a particular reason for reaching out to the souls will help you obtain better results. Of course, you can go out and hope to talk to an ancestor. However, without a purpose, you won't answer questions - nor will you be able to focus on this quest for too long – plus you risk running into unfriendly spirits that can take advantage of you. Perhaps you're unaware of having any unanswered questions, but you still feel complete to try Utesitta. If this is the case, consider why you want to do it. That said, the question doesn't have to be too specific. Here are some examples of intentions you can set:

"I have a question I need to be answered, and I wish to talk to my ancestors."

"There's a part of me that I fail to comprehend, and I need someone to provide me with clarity."

"Someone has come to me with a problem that they need help with, but I don't know how to help them."

"My pet dog is sick, and I need to know what to do about it."

"I am here and would like to talk to you about..."

Instructions:

1. Find a secluded place in nature and sit down.
2. Start paying attention to what is around you and how you experience your surroundings.
3. Look at the trees and the rocks. Observe the grass, the small animals, and the wind in the trees, and experience the sounds and the smells.
4. First, focus on one thing at a time, then move on to two, then focus on five things at once. The latter will be challenging, especially if you can't keep still.
5. Then, focus on your breathing, and bring your attention to yourself. If you're wearing a jacket, a cloak, or a hoodie, pull its edges closer to your body and put the hood on (if you have one).
6. You should now cease noticing anything from the outside. Concentrate on finding the core of your being. This could take 10-15 minutes to achieve and should be repeated for an hour or so.
7. Then, you can, once again, expand your attention outwards, except this time, you'll go past the boundary of your body. Try envisioning yourself experiencing your surroundings, but not as separate from you anymore.
8. At that point, you should become open to communicating with beings from other worlds.
9. You'll repeat this 5-12 times, depending on how many spirits you can reach and how long you're willing to seek answers or powers. Some entities will be less communicative, while others will readily help you.

Breathwork to Attain a Light Trance

Beginner Breathwork

To get into a light trance, you'll need to focus on your breathwork. Here is an easy way to get started. It's recommended to do this exercise in a sitting position. Avoid lying down, as having your legs firmly on the ground centers your mind during this. You want nature's energy to transcend your body and flow through it naturally.

Instructions:

1. Sit in a comfortable position and take a deep breath. While you're breathing in, count to four.
2. Count to four while holding your breath, and release it while counting to four again.
3. If you can, start extending the time while exhaling. If you cannot, stick to counting to four.
4. Repeat until you start reaching a deeper level of consciousness. You'll feel this when you sense your consciousness leaving you.
5. Let it happen automatically. Sit and let your breathing take over.
6. You should lose awareness of your body like it doesn't exist anymore. Only your soul exists - and it's now free to travel and communicate with other souls.
7. While the purpose of this light exercise isn't spiritual communication, if you encounter any other spirits, feel free to talk to them. If not, don't worry. For now, reaching the light trance is a perfectly acceptable outcome.

Heart Opening Breathwork

This simple breathing exercise will help you focus on your breathing and facilitate entering into a light trance.

Instructions:

1. Stand on the ground (preferably in a quiet place in nature).
2. Close your eyes and open your heart while feeling nature's grounding effects.
3. Take a deep breath and release. Repeat a couple of times until you're ready to visualize.

4. When ready, imagine a vast world in your mind's eye. This world is unseen to your eyes, but it slowly reveals itself to you.
5. Keep breathing deeply and releasing your breath slowly. Feel the strength of nature around you in the new world. Feel the life that flows through it all.

Chapter 8: Runic Magic and Divination

Runes are ancient symbols that had several purposes throughout the history of Norse Paganism - and this chapter will uncover all of them. You'll see how their use evolved from complex communication instruments to simple divination tools. You'll also find plenty of guides on selecting, consecrating, casting, and working with runes.

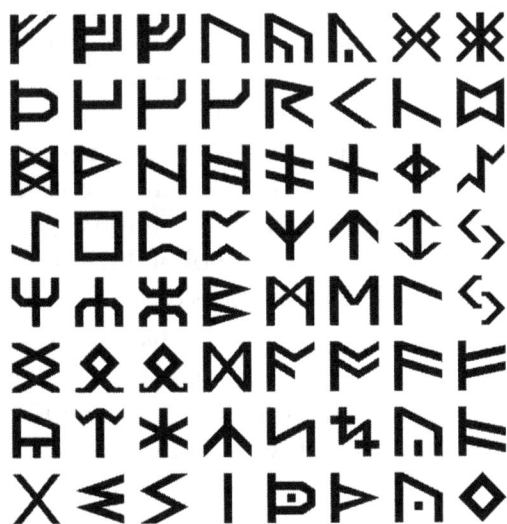

Examples of runes.[19]

The History of Runes

The information gained through historical records and Norse lore suggests that the runes were used predominantly as communication tools by ancient Germanic tribes. The earliest known evidence of runic writing comes from a carving that dates back to 400 C.E. When the Germanic pagans began to use the runes as letters (known as staves), they organized them into an alphabet. However, for the ancient Norse, the meaning of each stave wasn't as simple as the meaning of letters in most of today's languages. According to their beliefs, each rune symbolizes an aspect of life, a specific form of or a universal thought. The runes were used only by the most educated tribe members. They employed the runes to record events and prophecies affecting their community or to exchange information and forge alliances with the living and spirits.

In Old Norse, the primary meaning of the term rune is "enigma" or "a covert message." They believed that runes had magical properties which allowed people to send and receive messages from higher beings, inducing the deities, ancestral spirits, animals, and magical objects. The ancient Norse also believed that runes could unlock the secrets behind future events.

In the Norse alphabet, each rune was named after what it traditionally represented magically and spiritually. The earliest record shows that the staves were initially etched into stone tablets, which stood as a testimony to a particular tribe's achievements. As their knowledge of the runes advanced, Norse people began to inscribe them on small pieces of bone, stone, wood, or metal and carry them wherever they went so they could use them for different purposes. How each rune is depicted depends on how their name sounds and which letter they represent in the Norse alphabet. For example, the Tiwaz rune is shown as an upward-pointed arrow. This depicts the rune as the symbol of Tyr, the Norse god of war, known for his habit of traveling across the sky.

The runic alphabet is called "Futhark," which is an abbreviation of the runes Fehu, Uruz, Thurisaz, Ansuz, Raidho, and Kennaz. These were the first six runes of the oldest known runic alphabet, the Elder Futhark. This alphabet contains 24 runes, which were equivalent to a large number of letters in the Old English language. Elder Futhark is still used today for divination. The runes in this alphabet are divided into three Aetts, which are governed by three of the most powerful Norse deities, Freyr, Heimdall, and Tyr. Each aett also represents a specific stage in life - an early success, a failure, and prosperity in spite of life's hindrances.

The Meaning of Runes

The runes of the Elder Futhark have several meanings, often open to the reader's interpretation. That said, here are the aspects of life each rune is associated with, alongside their symbols.

ᚠ - Fehu

Pronounced "FAY-hoo," the name of this rune is translated as "cattle." Fehu can indicate abundance, material gain, wealth, luck, hope, property, and fortune. It can also symbolize the fulfillment of dreams and goals in the different aspects of life.

ᚢ - Uruz

Pronounced "OO-rooz," Uruz means "wild ox." Like this sacred animal, the rune is associated with willpower, strength, courage, perseverance, endurance, vitality, good times, and health. It is believed that Uruz has the power to shape one's destiny.

ᚦ - Thurisaz

Pronounced "THUR-ee-sazh," this rune in English means "giant." It symbolizes the hammer of Thor, protection, defense, disruptive forces, attack, or danger. Thurisaz can also mean that you must alter your life course to obtain divine empowerment.

ᚨ - Ansuz

Pronounced "AHN-sooz," the name of this rune can be translated as "revelation." It is associated with the Norse god Odin and his communication skills. Due to this, the rune depicts mental capacity, the mouth, and organs needed for speech. It can also symbolize other Norse deities you can communicate with through messages and insight.

ᚱ - Raidho

Pronounced "Rah-EED-ho," this rune means a "journey on horseback" in English. It can point to any form of movement, the conscious decision to work for your goals, progress in life, spiritual growth, and new perspectives.

ᚲ - Kenaz

Pronounced "KEN-ahz," Kenaz is a Norse term for ulcer. It can also mean torch, enlightenment, transformation, purpose, passion, or insight.

Many see the rune as a sign of a higher calling toward following one's dreams. Kenaz can also mean you can't let outside influences affect your life.

X - Gebo

Pronounced "GHEB-o," this rune is translated as "gift." It's seen as a sign of gratitude or the need to exchange something through offerings. Practitioners use Gebo to obtain assistance, blessings, partnership, service, or luck through acts of generosity and charity.

P - Wunjo

Pronounced "WOON-yo," this rune symbolizes joy and well-being. It can mean the fulfillment of dreams and a state of contentment. However, Wunjo can also mean that your happiness may be threatened by an impending change. Through loss and tests of strength, the rune enables you to maintain the ability to grow and thrive.

H - Hagalaz

Pronounced "HA-ga-lah," this rune is translated as "hail." It denotes difficulties that could halt or delay your plans. It can also refer to external input or nature's destructive influence. Despite the latter, Hagalaz can change one's life for the better.

+ - Naudhiz

Pronounced "NOWD-heez," Naudhiz means "need" in English. It can also highlight resistance, difficulty in thriving, lacking, or distress. It typically symbolizes the necessity to overcome a hurdle, the embodiment of your wishes, and the need to pay attention to your problems and unfulfilled desires.

I - Isa

Pronounced "EE-sa," this rune is translated as "ice." It symbolizes a hasty period of stillness when everything stops so you can see the changes you need to make. Isa is the key to successful self-renewal as it keeps you from following the same old patterns and remaining stuck.

ら - Jera

Pronounced "YARE-a," Jera sounds almost identical to its English translation - year. This rune represents harvest, the cycle of life and nature, rewards for hard work, and the end of an era. It also symbolizes new beginnings, opportunities for growth, and gathering abundance and wisdom.

ᛇ - Eihwaz

Pronounced "AY-wahz," this rune is translated as "yew." According to Norse mythology, the yew tree embodies supreme wisdom. Its symbol represents ways to uncover the mysteries of life, connect to the sacred divine energy and knowledge, and find inspiration, stability, and stability.

ᛈ - Perthro

Pronounced "PER-thro," Perthro conveys fate, prophecy, mysticism, and the occult. It can also symbolize fertility, self-awareness, and new opportunities to raise your fortune. This rune is a hint that your future depends on your current choices.

ᛉ - Algiz

Pronounced "AL-geez," this rune means "elk." This animal is associated with good luck, protection, courage, and spiritual awakening. It's a cue that you must tap into your intuition to find the connection to your higher self.

ᛊ - Sowilo

Pronounced "So-WEE-lo," Sowilo is translated as "Sun." It embodies vitality, abundance, solace, motivation, and joy. Whatever obstacles you face in life, this rune provides reassurance that you'll overcome them.

ᛏ - Tiwaz

Pronounced "TEE-wahz," this means "the god Thor." It conveys all the attributes of this Norse deity - including boldness, leadership, honor, divine strength, and courage. It can also depict your ability to make sacrifices and thrive despite the hurdles you face.

ᛒ - Berkano

Pronounced "BER-Kah-no," Berkano is translated as "birch" or "the birch goddess." It is associated with rebirth, fertility, and new beginnings. The rune can also point to the potential for growth and finding creative ways to begin anew after a challenging experience.

ᛖ - Ehwaz

Pronounced "EH-wahz," this rune means "horse." In Norse mythology, this animal is the symbol of trust. Besides this, the rune can symbolize companionship, faith in your progress, and partnership. It can also represent animal instinct, needing help, or wanting to move forward with your life.

ᛗ - Mannaz

Pronounced "MAN-Naz," Mannaz is the equivalent of the English word "man." The rune embodies humanity, mortality, and the balance between life and death. It can also symbolize human values and skills you develop throughout your life.

ᛚ - Laguz

Pronounced "LAH-gooz," this rune has several meanings. Laguz is primarily associated with water and fluidity, inner awareness, the unknown, and potential. It can also denote dreams, imagination, and having an open heart even through difficult times.

ᛜ - Ingwaz

Pronounced "ING-wahz," this rune is named after the god of Ingwaz. Its meaning is tied to new beginnings and unveiling one's potential by harnessing new energies, ancestral wisdom, or using sexuality. It also embodies peace, well-being, and spiritual growth.

ᛟ - Othala

Pronounced "OH-tha-la," this rune means "inheritance" in English. It's associated with heritage, ancestral wisdom, nobility, homecoming, property, and hidden talents. It can also suggest that your values lie in your legacy and connection to your community.

ᛞ - Dagaz

Pronounced "DAH-gahz," Dagaz is a Norse term for "day." It embodies inspiration, the possibility of awakening, hope, balance, changes at the beginning of the day, and the beginning of a new cycle. It can also denote spiritual growth, happiness, clarity, and self-awareness.

Runic Divination

According to the Eddic poem "Havamal," the runes were revealed to people by Odin himself. He uncovered the runes and their power during his ordeal while spending nine days and nights hanging from Yggdrasil. After the ninth night, he looked down, saw the runes, and they told him how to free himself. Realizing that the runes held even more wisdom than he possessed, Odin shared them with the other gods and goddesses. He taught them their meaning and how to use them, and, in turn, they passed on this knowledge to the people.

Prophesying future outcomes with runes (the practice known as rune casting) is one of the easiest divinatory methods. Similarly to Tarot readings, the runes are tossed or laid on a flat surface and then interpreted. The runes can be cast either randomly or in a specific pattern, in which case each rune has a particular purpose. Runic divination can only get you answers to simple questions to help you get a clearer picture of your future. It's not fortune-telling, and it won't give you specific answers. While the runes can reveal different influences related to your inquiries, they'll never show you a specific time of the day when something will happen. The runes denote the gateway to your subconscious through your intuition. By tapping into your subconscious and using it to decipher the runic symbols in front of you, you'll be able to find the answers already in your subconscious.

In the olden days, the runes were symbols carved on small sticks made from branches of nut-bearing trees. Traditionally, the runes were cast randomly on a piece of white cloth after a small ritual. This entailed the rune caster saying a quick prayer to the gods or spirits they asked to help interpret the results and looking up to the sky while tossing the runes in front of them. They would then interpret the results according to their preferences and traditions.

Selecting Your Runes

Nowadays, you can buy pre-made runes and entire rune-casting kits. They can be made from stone, wood, or even crystals. Crystals carry their own intrinsic magical energy but can be infused with your power or that of nature. You can also make your own rune set. This will foster a stronger connection between your energy and the runes, making it easier for your intuition to pick up the meaning of the runes. Whether you buy or create your own runes, selecting the right ones is crucial for making them work for you.

Here is how to select your rune kit:

1. Place your hands over the runes and see if you have any reaction to them.
2. Listen to your gut - it will sense the runes you have some connection to.
3. If you feel drawn to the runes, pick some of them up (or all of them in a pouch or box) and try to feel their energy.
4. These are the right ones for you if you feel a clear connection to the runes.

Consecrating Your Runes

After creating or selecting them, you must consecrate your runes. This will help you connect with the runes before using them for divination. You'll need a strong focus to do this, so make sure you aren't too preoccupied with other things to concentrate on your task. Here is a beginner-friendly way to consecrate your runes:

1. Place the runes in front of you and a candle beside them on your altar or table.
2. Light the candle and focus on its flame while you take a few deep breaths to help you focus.
3. Pick up a rune, recite its name aloud, and pass it over the candle flame.
4. Repeat with the rest of the runes.
5. When you have finished, put the runes in a protective bag or box to keep them away from negative influences until you need to use them.

Casting and Interpreting The Runes

Here is a simple way to cast and interpret the runes:

1. Place a white cloth on your altar, table, or another surface you want to work on.
2. Formulate a question in your mind. For starters, ask questions that can be answered with a "Yes" or "No." These will only confirm what you already know in your subconscious - but will help you get the hang of listening to your intuition.
3. Take the bag or box of runes and toss the runes onto the cloth.
4. Look up towards the sky, and if you wish to call on a guide to help you interpret the runes, do it.
5. Then, look down at the runes and try to interpret their meaning. Try interpreting one rune at a time.
6. The symbolic meaning of a prophecy depends entirely on your interpretation. For example, Jera means "harvest," which can be interpreted as reaping the rewards of your work.
7. However, when it comes up, you'll need to wonder whether you're expecting rewards for any work you've done recently.
8. If the first thought you have when looking at Jera is that you're looking into a new opportunity instead of a reward - then this is

probably the correct meaning at that time.

Reading a Rune Spread

Once you've mastered reading one rune, you can move on to a three-rune spread. Here is how to do that:

1. Take a deep breath, take out three runes, and lay them in front of you in a horizontal line.
2. The middle one reflects your current situation and actions.
3. The one on the left showcases past influences.
4. While the rune on the right illustrates the most likely future outcome of your present actions.

Creating Your Own Charms and Spells

While you can use pre-existing charms and spells, creating your own will make them even more powerful. However, to do this, you'll need to understand how the position of the runes will impact their effectiveness in a charm or spell. Here are the positions to consider:

- **Direct position** - Indicates their most indicative values and symbolism.
- **Inverted runes:** Related to the direct meaning of the runes but in a somewhat exaggerated manner.
- **Mirror position:** Use them to make bind runes, but exercise precaution because they have the power to trap energy and provide very little in return.

When making your own spells and charms, you must work on your visualization technique and sharpen your intuition as much as possible. Here is how to do it:

1. Visualize your intent until it becomes a word you can see in front of you. One simple word can be so powerful that it is enough to take effect. You can create rune spells or charms from composite words if you're more confident.
2. Alternatively, you can inscribe entire spells into your runic magical tool. For example, you can use spells for protection, fertility, or summoning guides.
3. Repeat visualizing the rune you're using until you can do it confidently. The easier it's for you to do this, the more effective your magic will be.

4. If you have trouble visualizing runes, pick one from a table before you and try to imagine it with your eyes closed. Try with black and white images first, then move on to colored ones.
5. When you've mastered imagining the runes' shape, you can add textures or images to their forms. Try finding images that best represent their core meaning, and focus on these when trying to visualize them.
6. Once you can connect to their core meaning, you'll be able to memorize the details you'll need when trying to create the runes that best describe your intention.
7. Next, depending on your purpose, select the material you will use. If you have a long-term goal, you'll need something sturdy, like stone or wood. If you have a short-term goal, paper will suffice.
8. Don't forget to consider whether you want to create a spell, a talisman, or something else. For example, if you're making a protective charm for yourself, you'll need to carry it around to take effect. In this case, you can create a pendant for a necklace, which you can take wherever you go.
9. However, if you need protection for your home, an art piece to hang on your walls would be a more suitable choice.
10. Carve the rune into the desired surface while sitting in a calming atmosphere. You can meditate beforehand to relax your mind and let it focus on the task.
11. You can also repeat the meditation when you have finished your work. Don't forget to thank your guides for their help.
12. Keep the rune somewhere you can see it whenever you need to draw on its power. Once you've reached your goal, you can destroy the rune.

Chapter 9: Bindrunes and Sigils

The use of symbols and sigils has been an integral part of human spirituality and magical practices for millennia. In Norse paganism, the use of bindrunes holds a significant place in both historical and modern practices. Bindrunes, also known as rune sigils, are symbols created by combining two or more runic letters to form a unique design with a specific meaning and purpose.

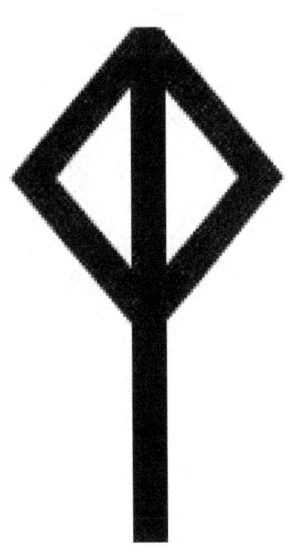

Ing bindrune.[30]

Historically, bindrunes were used in ancient Germanic and Norse cultures to convey personal or family identity, protection, and magical intent. For instance, Viking warriors would carve bindrunes into their weapons or shields to imbue them with the power of the runes and protect themselves in battle. They were also used in everyday life to ward off negative energies or to promote prosperity and good luck.

Today, bindrunes continue to play an essential role in modern magical practices and Norse paganism. They are used in spells, meditations, and ritual practices to manifest intentions, protect oneself, and connect with the energies of the runes. Additionally, creating a personal bindrune can be a powerful tool for self-expression, personal growth, and spiritual development.

This chapter will provide an in-depth look into the intricacies of bindrunes and their significance in Norse paganism. Plus, you'll learn how to create and consecrate your bindrune using elemental energy and various activation methods. This exploration of bindrunes will provide you with the tools needed to create a personalized symbol of power that can help you manifest your intentions, connect with the energies of the runes, and deepen your spiritual practice.

Types of Bindrunes

Bindrunes are classified into different types based on factors such as the type of runes used, their design, and their intended purpose or function.

1. Overlapping Bindrunes

Overlapping bindrunes, also known as intersecting bindrunes, are a type of bindrune that involve overlapping two or more runes to create a new symbol. These runes are carefully selected based on their individual meanings and properties and are combined in a way that creates a new, more complex symbol with a specific purpose or intention.

One example of an overlapping bindrune is the Vegvisir, often used as a protective symbol in Norse paganism. The Vegvisir was created by overlapping several different runes, including the Othala, Algiz, and Isa runes. The Othala rune is a straight line with two diagonal lines branching off it, while the Algiz rune looks like a diamond shape with two diagonal lines branching off the top. Finally, the Isa rune looks like an upright straight line.

When these runes overlap, they create a complex symbol that provides guidance and protection to the wearer. Overlapping bindrunes can also be used for other purposes, such as healing, manifestation, and creativity.

2. Stacked Bindrunes

Stacked bindrunes, on the other hand, are a type of linear bindrune that involve the combination of two or more runes stacked on top of each other. This type is often used in modern magic and can be seen in various symbols, logos, and designs.

One example of a stacked bindrune is the modern Bluetooth symbol, created by overlapping the runes for "H" and "B" to create a new, more complex symbol. Stacked bindrunes are often used for specific purposes, such as communication, protection, or manifestation, and are carefully crafted to include the appropriate runes and symbolism for the intended purpose.

3. Linear Bindrunes

Linear bindrunes combine two or more runes in a linear fashion along the same axis. This can involve overlapping the runes or placing them side-by-side. When creating a linear bindrune, the specific runes used and their placement are important considerations. Each rune has a specific meaning and energy associated with it, and the combination of these energies can create a powerful symbol with a specific purpose. For example, the Odin bindrune combines the Othala, Dagaz, and Isa runes in a linear fashion. The Othala rune represents inheritance and property, the Dagaz rune represents transformation and new beginnings, while the Isa rune represents stillness and focus. When these three runes are combined linearly, they create a powerful symbol that can help the user manifest new beginnings and focus on achieving their goals.

4. Stave Bindrunes

Stave bindrunes, or radial bindrunes, combine multiple runes stemming from a common center point. This type of bindrune is commonly used for protection or as an amulet. An example of a stave bindrune is the Helm of Awe, which combines the Algiz, Raido, and Othala runes. The Algiz rune represents protection and defense, the Raido rune represents movement and journey, while the Othala rune represents inheritance and property. When these three runes are combined radially, they create a powerful symbol that provides protection and security to the wearer.

In addition, some bindrunes are designed to function as sigils, symbols charged with magical intent to achieve a specific outcome. The design can be personalized by combining specific runes uniquely and meaningfully while incorporating additional lines, curves, or symbols into the basic structure. The sigil bindrune is then charged with magical intent through various methods, like visualization, meditation, or ritualistic practices.

Sigil bindrunes are used in magic and ritual to manifest a desired outcome, like protection, success, or love. They can be created for personal use or shared with others to invoke a specific energy or intention. Once charged, the sigil bindrune can be used in various ways, such as drawing it on a piece of paper or carving it onto a piece of wood or stone.

Some practitioners also carry the sigil bindrune with them or incorporate it into their personal altar or sacred space.

The power of a sigil bindrune lies in its ability to combine the energies of multiple runes into a single symbol charged with a specific intent. The design can be adapted to suit the specific needs and desires of the practitioner, making it a highly personalized and effective tool in magic and ritual. However, the effectiveness of a sigil bindrune relies on the focus and intent of the practitioner, as well as their connection to the energy and symbolism of the runes used to create it.

Crafting Bindrunes: A Step-by-Step Guide

Crafting your own bindrune is a fun and creative process that can bring a sense of empowerment and help you with specific rituals in your practice. Before you start doodling runes on a piece of paper, you need to understand the meanings of each individual rune. Mixing the wrong ones can lead to unintended consequences or even nullify the intended outcome. Don't let this intimidate you, though. The best way to learn is by doing, and practice makes perfect. Start with a simple two-rune sigil for a short-term goal, and don't be afraid to experiment. Look at other bind runes made by experts, analyze them, and see how they work. There are many runic alphabets to choose from, but as a beginner, the Elder Futhark is the most common one to start with. Once you've gained sufficient knowledge of runes, follow this step-by-step guide. Remember, the possibilities are endless, so let your creativity flow and have fun!

1. Visualize the Desired Outcome

Before you start picking runes, take some time to visualize what you want to achieve and the steps you need to take to get there. Once you have a clear picture of your goal, you can choose the runes that correspond to your desired outcome. Remember to pay attention to the meanings of each individual rune and how they can work together to create a powerful sigil.

Let's say you want to create a bindrune for success in your job search. The first step would be to visualize what success in your job search looks like. Perhaps it's landing your dream job, or maybe it's simply getting more interviews. Once you have a clear picture of your desired outcome, consider what qualities or attributes you need to succeed. For example, you might need confidence, communication skills, or networking abilities. Then, you can choose runes representing those qualities and combine them into a bindrune representing your goal.

2. Select the Runes

When selecting the runes for your bind rune, take some time to really consider each one and its meanings. This step is crucial as each rune you choose will impact your bind rune's overall intention and effectiveness. One helpful tip is to research the runes and their meanings. Take some time to understand the symbolism behind each rune and how they have been used historically. This will help you to make more informed decisions when selecting which runes to include in your bind rune.

You should also avoid over-complicating things. For beginners, it's better to limit your choices to two or three runes, and even for more experienced practitioners, it's usually best to keep it simple with five at most. This way, you can ensure that each rune you include has a clear purpose and contributes to the overall goal of your bind rune.

For instance, if your goal is to get a new job, you could select the runes representing success, communication, and prosperity. In this case, you could choose the runes Raidho (symbolizing travel and journeys), Ansuz (representing communication and inspiration), and Fehu (meaning wealth and prosperity). Together, these three runes would create a bind rune that focuses on finding success and prosperity.

3. Create Your Design

Now that you have selected the runes that best fit your intention, it's time to create your own unique bind rune. Get a pen and paper and start drawing as many combinations as you can. Don't worry about making mistakes; this is a creative process, and there's no right or wrong way to do it. If you're feeling stuck, take a break and do something else to clear your mind. Sometimes the perfect design will come to you unexpectedly, like in a dream or while taking a walk. When you return to your sketches, pick the ones that resonate with you the most. Take a closer look to see if any hidden or reversed runes have appeared, as these can affect the purpose of your spell.

Continuing the example above, you can create a design for your bindrune by creating a horizontal line with the Raidho rune at the left end, the Ansuz rune at the center, and the Fehu rune at the right end. Or, to add an extra layer of meaning, the three runes could also be positioned vertically, with Raidho at the top, Ansuz in the middle, and Fehu at the bottom. This arrangement can represent a journey toward prosperity, with communication and inspiration playing a crucial role in achieving success.

4. Select the Material

Choosing the right material for your bind rune is an essential step of the process. The material you use can have a significant impact on the effectiveness of the bind rune. When selecting the material, you should consider the purpose of your bind rune and how you intend to use it. If you are creating it for a long-term goal, it's best to choose a material that can withstand the test of time, like stone or wood. These materials have been used for centuries in magical practices and are known for their durability. On the other hand, if your bind rune is for a short-term goal, regular paper or cardboard can suffice.

When selecting the material, you should also consider how you plan to use the bind rune. If you want to wear it as a necklace, you can use a small piece of wood or stone and attach a chain or a string to it. Alternatively, if you want to hang it on your wall, you can use a piece of canvas or paper and create a beautiful art piece. Whatever you choose, make sure it's practical and easy to carry or display.

Consecrating Your Bindrune

Before you jump into the process of consecrating your bindrune, you need to learn more about elemental energy and its significance. According to ancient beliefs, the elements of Earth, Air, Fire, and Water are the universe's building blocks, and each of these elements carries a unique energy that can be harnessed for magical purposes.

There are various methods of activation when it comes to consecrating your bindrune. One way is to engrave or draw your bindrune on a material associated with an element. For example, if you want to infuse your bindrune with the energy of Fire, you can carve it on a piece of wood and then burn it in a fire to release the energy.

Another way is to create a ritual with elemental symbols and tools. You can use candles, incense, and crystals to represent the different elements and create a sacred space for your ritual. For example, you can light a green candle for Earth, a yellow candle for Air, a red candle for Fire, and a blue candle for Water to symbolize the four elements and their energies.

You can also charge your bindrune with elemental energy through visualization and meditation. This involves visualizing the energy of the element you want to infuse into your bindrune and meditating on it. For example, suppose you want to charge your bindrune with the energy of water. In that case, you can visualize yourself standing under a waterfall, feeling the cool water washing over you and filling your bindrune with its energy.

Consecrating your bindrune is an essential part of the ritual in Norse Paganism. It is believed that the act of consecration imbues your bindrune with divine power and makes it a sacred object. By doing so, you're inviting the deities to bless and empower your bindrune, increasing the effectiveness of your spell.

Putting Your Bindrune to Work

Now that you have created and consecrated your bindrune, it's time to put it to work. Depending on your intention and creativity, there are numerous ways to use your bindrune. You can wear it as jewelry, carry it in your pocket, or hang it in your workspace. You can incorporate it into your daily meditation or place it on your altar. The possibilities are endless, and the key is to find what works best for you and your purpose. Using your bindrune consistently invites its energy and power into your life, creating a potent tool for manifestation and transformation. Here are some ideas that you can consider:

- Try creating a necklace or bracelet with your bindrune, and wear it as a talisman to carry its energy with you throughout the day.
- Draw or paint your bindrune on a canvas or piece of wood, and hang it in your home or workspace as a constant reminder of your intention.
- You can carve your bindrune into a candle and light it whenever you need a boost of energy or a reminder of your intention.
- Meditate on your bindrune, visualizing its energy flowing through your body and bringing your intention to life.
- If you have an altar or sacred space, you can place your bindrune on it as a focal point for your intention.
- Incorporate your bindrune into other spellwork, using its energy to enhance your spells.
- If you keep a journal or grimoire, you can include your bindrune in it as a record of your intention and a reminder of your magic.
- Create a small bag filled with herbs, crystals, and other items that correspond to your intention, and include your bindrune in it for added energy.

- Use your bindrune as a symbol in tarot readings or other divination practices, gaining insight into your intention and its manifestation.

Bindrunes and sigils are powerful tools in Norse paganism. They provide you with a way to focus and manifest your intentions. When working with bindrunes, the key is to select the right runes, design a unique symbol, and consecrate it properly, to create a powerful talisman that reflects your deepest desires. While this chapter provides a solid foundation for creating your own bindrunes and sigils, there is always more to learn and explore. Don't be afraid to experiment with different materials, symbols, and techniques to find what works best for you. Remember, the true power of bind runes comes from within.

Chapter 10: Stadhagaldr: Runic Yoga

Runes hold a sacred place in Norse Paganism, representing not just a system of divination but also powerful symbols of the gods and the cosmos. The Nordic tradition of runes is deeply connected to the primal forces of nature, the mysteries of life, and the spiritual realm. Over time, runes have evolved from their original use as an alphabet into a potent tool for personal transformation and spiritual growth. One way to harness the runes' transformative power is through the practice of Runic Yoga. Runic Yoga, or Stadhagaldr, is a fusion of yoga and runic symbolism that allows you to deepen your connection to the divine and unlock your full potential.

It involves using physical postures that embody the energy and meaning of each of the twenty-four runes of the Elder Futhark. Each posture represents a specific rune, and as you move through the postures, you connect with the energies of the runes, creating a powerful transformation within yourself. This practice has been used for centuries as a tool for spiritual growth. This chapter will explore the concept of Runic Yoga, its origins, and how it can be used to deepen your connection to the divine and unlock your full potential. You'll learn about the many benefits of this practice, the different runic postures, and how to practice it.

The Birth of Stadhagaldr

The origins of Stadhagaldr can be traced back to the 1930s, a time when interest in ancient runic signs was at its peak. Linguists, mystics, and practitioners sought to find practical applications for the ancient symbols. Two German scientists, Friedrich Bernhard Marby and Siegfried Adolf Kummer, believed that the runes were instructions for meditative gymnastics, similar to hatha yoga.

Marby and Kummer's theory even had a scientific basis, grounded in real archaeological finds, including the ancient German magical figures of *alrau*ns, which were made as charms, and the sculptural images from the famous golden horns found in South Jutland. These images depict people in poses imitating particular runes, and it was the golden horns from Gallehus that inspired the development of runic yoga.

Marby believed that with the help of "rune gymnastics" or "rune dance," one could access areas inaccessible to the perception of an ordinary person, come into contact with higher forces, and influence cosmic processes. Kummer believed that runic magic allowed you to control energy flows from space by taking the correct runic posture and adjusting perception with the help of special sounds.

The name *Stadhagaldr* comes from the Old Norse words "*stadha*," which means to stand, and "*galdr*," which means to chant or to enchant. Although the use of certain poses, gestures, and the chanting of runes were not invented by Marby or Kummer, they rediscovered the forgotten tradition of Norse magic.

Stadhagaldr's unique combination of physical and spiritual practices makes it a powerful tool for personal growth and transformation. It is a significant part of the Norse pagan heritage, reflecting the deep connection between the Norse people and the natural world. Today, Stadhagaldr continues to be an important part of the modern pagan community, offering practitioners a way to connect with the divine and explore the power of the runes.

Benefits of Runic Yoga

The practice of Stadhagaldr is deeply rooted in Norse Paganism, reflecting the profound connection between the ancient Norse people and the natural world. One of the most significant benefits of Runic Yoga is its ability to help practitioners tap into the transformative power of the runes.

In Norse Paganism, runes are regarded as sacred symbols that represent the primal forces of nature, the mysteries of life, and the spiritual realm. Through the practice of Runic Yoga, individuals can deepen their connection to these powerful symbols, unlock their full potential, and access hidden knowledge.

Another benefit of Runic Yoga is its ability to promote physical health and well-being. Traditional yoga postures are well-known for their ability to increase flexibility, build strength, and improve overall fitness. When combined with the transformative power of the runes, these physical benefits can be enhanced even further, promoting a deeper sense of connection between the body, mind, and spirit.

In addition to its physical benefits, Runic Yoga is also a powerful tool for mental and emotional well-being. The deep breathing and meditation involved can calm the mind and promote relaxation. This can be particularly helpful for individuals who suffer from stress, anxiety, or depression, as it provides a way to connect with the divine and find peace and balance amidst the chaos of everyday life.

For those interested in exploring their spirituality, Runic Yoga can be an excellent way to connect with the divine and explore the mysteries of the universe. In Norse Paganism, the natural world is considered sacred, and runes are seen as a way to connect with the spiritual forces that govern the cosmos. Through Runic Yoga, individuals can connect with these forces, gaining a deeper understanding of the universe and their place within it.

Another one of the unique benefits of Runic Yoga is its ability to connect individuals with their ancestral heritage. The practice is deeply rooted in Norse Paganism, reflecting the ancient wisdom and knowledge of the Norse people. For individuals who have a connection to their Norse heritage, Runic Yoga can be an excellent way to explore their cultural roots and connect with their ancestors.

Different Runic Postures

Runic postures are physical positions that correspond to the various runic symbols and are believed to represent the primal forces of nature, the mysteries of life, and the spiritual realm. Each posture is designed to activate specific energies and promote personal transformation. There are a variety of runic postures, each with its unique benefits and symbolism. Some postures are designed to promote strength and stability, while others are intended to cultivate mental and emotional balance. Below are some of the most common runic postures practiced in Stadhagaldr.

1. Fehu - Cattle or Wealth

The Fehu posture is a powerful runic posture representing cattle or wealth and is associated with abundance and prosperity. This posture can be performed by combining several traditional yoga asanas, including Tadasana (Mountain Pose) and Utkatasana (Chair Pose). To perform the Fehu posture, follow these steps:

- Stand straight with your feet hip-width apart, toes facing forward.
- Ground your feet firmly on the floor, and engage your core muscles.
- Lift your arms above your head, with your palms facing each other.
- Interlace your fingers, and stretch your arms up toward the sky.
- Inhale deeply and, as you exhale, bend your knees, and sink into a squatting position.
- Keep your arms stretched above your head, and continue interlacing your fingers.
- Hold the position for a few breaths, focusing on grounding and connecting with the earth.
- On your next inhale, rise up out of the squat, straightening your legs and lifting your heels off the ground.
- Hold the position for a few breaths.
- Lower your heels back to the ground on your next exhale, releasing your hands to your sides.

The Fehu posture combines the grounding and stability of Tadasana with the forward motion of Utkatasana to create a posture that promotes both strength and abundance. By sinking into a squatting position and rising onto the balls of your feet, the Fehu posture activates the energy of abundance and prosperity, helping manifest material and physical well-being.

The Fehu posture shares some similarities with the traditional Chinese practice of Qigong. Both practices combine physical movements and breathwork to promote physical and material well-being, and both draw on the ancient wisdom of their respective cultures.

2. Uruz - Aurochs or Strength

The Uruz posture is a potent runic posture utilized in Runic Yoga, symbolizing the primal strength of the wild ox and associated with vitality, courage, and passion. The posture requires combining traditional yoga asanas, including Virabhadrasana I (Warrior I) and Utkatasana (Chair Pose). Here is how to perform the Uruz posture:

- Stand straight with your feet hip-width apart, toes facing forward.
- Move your right foot back a step into a lunge position, bending your left knee at a 90-degree angle while keeping your right leg straight.
- Lift your arms above your head with palms facing each other.
- Inhale deeply and exhale as you sink deeper into the lunge, lowering your hips towards the ground.
- While keeping your arms stretched above your head, lift through your fingertips, and focus on the sensation of strength and power.
- Hold the position for a few breaths.
- Inhale and rise up out of the lunge, straightening both legs and lowering your arms to your sides.
- Repeat the posture on the opposite side by moving your left foot back a step into a lunge position and lifting your arms above your head.

By combining the traditional yoga asanas of Warrior, and Chair Pose, the Uruz posture creates a powerful and grounding experience that allows you to connect with the primal strength of the wild ox. This posture shares similarities with other yoga practices that focus on strength and stability, such as the warrior series in Vinyasa yoga. However, the incorporation of runic symbolism in the Uruz posture adds an additional layer of meaning and intention to the practice, allowing for a deeper exploration of the spiritual and energetic aspects of the posture.

3. Thurisaz - Thorn or Protection

The Thurisaz posture is a potent runic posture utilized in Runic Yoga, representing the power of the thorn or the hammer of the thunder god Thor. It is associated with protection, courage, and the ability to overcome obstacles. To perform the Thurisaz posture, a combination of traditional yoga asanas, including Virabhadrasana II (Warrior II) and Utthita Trikonasana (Extended Triangle Pose), are required. Follow these steps:

- Begin in a standing position with your feet hip-width apart and your arms at your sides.
- Move your left foot back three to four feet, with your left toes turned out at a 45-degree angle.
- Align your right heel with the center arch of your left foot.
- Inhale deeply, then exhale as you bend your right knee, keeping it directly above your ankle.
- As you exhale, turn your torso to the right, extending your arms straight out from your shoulders, palms facing down.
- Engage your core muscles and focus your gaze over your right hand, imagining yourself wielding the power of Thor's hammer.
- Inhale deeply, and as you exhale, reach forward with your right hand, extending it past your right knee and reaching toward the ground.
- Extend your left arm up toward the ceiling, keeping both arms in line with your shoulders.
- Hold the posture for several breaths, focusing on the energy of protection, courage, and overcoming obstacles.
- Inhale and straighten your right knee, then release your arms and step your left foot forward to return to the standing position.
- Repeat the posture on the opposite side by stepping your right foot back and turning your torso to the left.

The Thurisaz posture in Runic Yoga shares similarities with traditional Warrior II and Extended Triangle Pose in Hatha yoga. However, incorporating runic symbolism and intentionality adds a deeper layer of meaning and purpose to the practice, allowing for a more holistic and transformative experience.

4. Ansuz - Odin or Wisdom

The Ansuz posture in Runic Yoga represents divine communication and clarity of thought. It combines traditional yoga asanas such as Tadasana (Mountain Pose) and Ardha Uttanasana (Half Forward Bend) with runic symbolism to encourage introspection and powerful communication. Here are the steps to perform the Ansuz posture:

- Stand tall with your feet hip-width apart and your arms at your sides.
- Take a deep breath in, then exhale as you bring your arms up overhead, interlacing your fingers and pointing your index fingers toward the sky.
- Inhale deeply again, then exhale as you lean to the right, keeping your arms straight and your hands interlaced.
- Hold the posture for a few breaths, imagining the breath of life flowing through you and filling you with inspiration and clarity of thought.
- Inhale deeply and return to center, then exhale and repeat the posture, this time leaning to the left.
- Release your hands and bring them back to your sides.
- Inhale deeply, then exhale as you lunge forward at the hips, keeping your back flat and your gaze forward.
- As you exhale, imagine yourself speaking with confidence and power, allowing the energy of the Ansuz rune to flow through you.
- Hold the posture for several breaths, then inhale deeply and return to the standing position.
- Repeat the posture a few more times, focusing on the intention of clarity of thought, inspiration, and powerful communication.

The Ansuz posture in Runic Yoga is similar to traditional yoga asanas like Mountain Pose and Half Forward Bend, which provide a grounding foundation while also encouraging introspection and communication. However, the addition of runic symbolism and intention-setting brings a deeper spiritual aspect to the practice. By incorporating the energy of the Ansuz rune, practitioners can connect with the divine and tap into their own power of speech and communication.

5. Raidho - Wheel or Journey

The Raidho posture in Runic Yoga is dynamic and energetic, representing life's journey. It is believed to enhance physical and mental strength and promote balance and harmony within both the body and mind. This posture is particularly useful for those seeking to embark on a new journey or make significant life changes. To practice this posture, follow these steps:

- Begin by standing with your feet shoulder-width apart and your arms raised above your head.
- Clasp your hands together tightly with your index fingers pointing upward.
- Take a deep breath and focus your intention on your journey, visualizing the path ahead of you.
- Exhale and begin to twist your torso to the right, keeping your arms and hands raised.
- Pivot your left foot on the ground to rotate your entire body.
- Hold this position for a few breaths, then inhale and return to center.
- Repeat the twisting motion to the left side, pivoting on your right foot this time.
- Focus on your breath and allow the energy of the Raidho rune to guide you.

The Raidho posture has similarities to several traditional yoga asanas, including the Twisting Chair Pose and the Warrior II Pose. Like these poses, the Raidho posture promotes strength, stability, and balance within the body. However, adding runic symbolism and intention-setting brings a unique aspect to the practice.

6. Kenaz - Torch or Illumination

Kenaz, the rune of torch or illumination, is associated with knowledge, creativity, and transformation. The Runic posture associated with Kenaz incorporates several yoga asanas that stimulate the nervous system and improve mental focus. This posture is often used to access deeper states of creativity and inspiration, making it a valuable tool for artists and writers. To perform the Kenaz posture, follow these steps:

- Begin by standing with your feet shoulder-width apart and your arms by your sides.
- Take a deep breath and raise your arms overhead, bringing your palms together in a prayer position.
- Inhale and lift your heels off the ground, balancing on the balls of your feet.
- Exhale and lower your heels, bringing your palms to your heart.

- As you inhale, extend your arms forward, keeping your palms together and your gaze focused on your fingertips.
- Exhale and slowly lower your arms back to your heart.
- Repeat steps 5 and 6 several times, allowing the movement to flow with your breath.
- As you continue to move, visualize the torch of Kenaz illuminating your inner creative spark and guiding you toward greater inspiration and understanding.

The Kenaz posture shares some similarities with traditional yoga practices such as Tree Pose (Vrikshasana) and Warrior I (Virabhadrasana I), as it requires balance and concentration. However, its unique combination of movements and focus on illumination sets it apart as a powerful tool for accessing creativity and insight.

Runic Yoga is a unique and powerful practice that combines physical postures, breathing techniques, and runic symbolism for personal growth and spiritual transformation. It is deeply rooted in Norse Paganism, reflecting the connection between nature and the Norse people. Through Runic Yoga, you can access the wisdom and strength of your ancestors, unlocking new levels of self-awareness and insight. The practice offers a pathway to a greater understanding of oneself and the world, unlocking one's full potential. The power of Runic Yoga should be honored and embraced for its transformative effects on people's lives. It is a potent tool that connects individuals to the divine power within and offers a pathway to deeper healing and creative inspiration.

Glossary of Terms

Asatru - A modern revival of Norse Paganism that focuses on the worship of the Aesir, the pantheon of gods and goddesses in Norse mythology. Followers of Asatru seek to connect with the natural world and the spirits of their ancestors through rituals, meditation, and personal devotion. It has gained popularity in recent decades as a way for people of Norse heritage or those drawn to the mythology and culture of the Vikings to connect with their ancestral roots.

Asgard - The realm of the Aesir gods, associated with war, strength, and wisdom.

Ancestor worship is honoring and communicating with deceased ancestors in pagan religions. It involves showing respect and gratitude toward one's ancestors by making offerings, performing rituals, and seeking their guidance and wisdom.

Alfheim - The realm of the light elves, associated with fertility, growth, and prosperity.

Blot - A ritual sacrifice or offering typically performed to honor the gods and goddesses in Norse Paganism. The ritual typically involves the sacrifice of an animal, which is then cooked and eaten as part of a communal feast. Other offerings, such as mead, ale, bread, or fruit, may also be given to the gods during the ceremony.

Eddas - The primary source of Norse mythology and pagan beliefs, consisting of the Poetic Edda and Prose Edda. The Poetic Edda is a collection of Old Norse poems that provides insight into the gods, heroes, and myths of Norse culture, while the Prose Edda, written by Snorri

Sturluson in the 13th century, is a guide to Norse mythology and poetic techniques.

Einherjar - The warriors chosen by Odin to fight alongside him in Valhalla. According to Norse mythology, the einherjar were chosen from those who died bravely in battle and were brought to Valhalla by the Valkyries.

Forn Siðr - Also known as Old Way or Old Norse Tradition, refers to the traditional religious practices of the ancient Norse people before the introduction of Christianity. It involves the veneration of deities such as Odin, Thor, and Freyja and the use of runes, magic, and ritual sacrifice. Forn Siðr is still practiced today by modern Heathens who seek to revive and reconstruct the traditions of their ancestors.

Futhark - The runic alphabet used in Norse Paganism, consisting of 24 letters divided into three groups of eight. The runes were used for writing inscriptions on various objects, such as weapons, amulets, and runestones, and they were also used for divination and magical purposes.

Gyðja - A female priestess in Norse Paganism who also leads rituals and provides spiritual guidance. Gyðjas were highly respected and highly esteemed for their knowledge, wisdom, and connection with the divine. They often served as healers, seers, and intermediaries between the gods and mortals.

Hávamál - A collection of Old Norse poems containing wisdom and advice attributed to the god Odin, often used as a guide for ethical behavior in Norse Paganism. It consists of 164 stanzas, each providing insight into various aspects of life, including hospitality, friendship, love, and honor. Hávamál also includes magical charms and spells that were believed to have protective powers.

Helheim - The realm of the dead, ruled by the goddess Hel and associated with death and decay.

Jötunn - A giant in Norse mythology, sometimes worshiped in Norse Paganism as a powerful and unpredictable force of nature.

Jotunheim - The realm of the giants, associated with chaos, unpredictability, and raw power.

Jörmungandr - Also known as the Midgard Serpent. In Norse mythology, Jörmungandr is a gigantic sea serpent, one of the three children of the god Loki and the giantess Angrboða. According to the legend, Jörmungandr grew so large that it could encircle the earth and hold onto its own tail. Jörmungandr was an arch-enemy of the god Thor, and their battles were said to be cataclysmic events that would shake the earth and the seas. In Norse mythology, it is said that during Ragnarok, the final battle, Jörmungandr and Thor would face each other in an epic showdown that would result in both of their deaths.

Landvættir - Nature spirits or guardians of the land in Norse Paganism, often associated with specific natural features such as mountains, rivers, or forests. They are often depicted as animal-like beings or anthropomorphic figures and were traditionally honored with offerings and rituals to ensure the land's and its inhabitants' well-being.

Midgard - The realm of humans, also known as Earth, where most myths and legends occur.

Mjölnir - The hammer of Thor, a symbol commonly used in Norse Paganism to represent strength, protection, and the power of the gods.

Níðstang - A pole inscribed with curses or insults, used in Norse Paganism as a way to bring shame or dishonor to an enemy or rival. The belief was that the curse would bring shame and dishonor upon the person targeted, causing them to lose social standing and respect within their community.

Niflheim - The realm of ice and mist, associated with darkness and coldness.

Nine Realms - The realms in Norse cosmology, including Asgard and Helheim, are inhabited by various gods, giants, and other supernatural beings.

Muspelheim - The realm of fire and heat, associated with destruction and creation.

Oath-taking - A solemn commitment often performed in Norse Paganism, in which an individual swears to uphold certain values or fulfill certain obligations.

Ragnarok - A series of catastrophic events that will ultimately lead to the end of the world. According to Norse mythology, Ragnarok will begin with a long and harsh winter known as "Fimbulwinter," during which the world will be plagued by natural disasters and wars.

Eventually, the final battle between the gods and the giants will take place, known as the Battle of Ragnarok. In this battle, many major gods and monsters will be killed, and the world as we know it will be destroyed. The god Odin will be killed by the giant wolf Fenrir, and Thor will die after killing the Midgard serpent.

After the battle, a new world will be born, and the few surviving gods and humans will start anew. This new world will be inhabited by a new generation of gods and humans who will live in peace and harmony. In Norse mythology, Ragnarok warns about the world's impermanence and the inevitability of change and renewal.

Runes - Symbols used in divination and magic in Norse Paganism, believed to possess spiritual and mystical power.

Seidr - A form of Norse magic often associated with women, involving the use of trance, ritual, and divination to communicate with spirits and affect the natural world. The practice of Seiðr was viewed with suspicion by some in Norse society, as it was associated with the use of manipulation and deception to achieve one's goals.

Svartalfheim - The realm of the dark elves and dwarves, associated with craftsmanship and hidden treasures.

The High One - A nickname for Odin, one of the primary gods in Norse Paganism, associated with wisdom, knowledge, and the pursuit of power.

Thurseblot - A winter solstice celebration in Norse Paganism involving sacrificing animals and making offerings to the giants and other forces of darkness. This festival involves the sacrifice of animals and the offering of mead or other beverages to the Jötnar.

Týr - A god associated with war and justice in Norse Paganism, often depicted as a one-handed warrior who sacrificed his hand to bind the giant wolf Fenrir.

Valhalla - A great hall in Asgard where fallen warriors are taken in Norse mythology and Paganism, presided over by Odin and his Valkyries.

Vanaheim - The realm of the Vanir gods, associated with fertility, prosperity, and magic.

Vanir - A group of gods associated with fertility and prosperity in Norse Paganism, often depicted as having close connections to the natural world.

Ve - The brother of Odin and Vili, who helped create the world in Norse mythology and Paganism and may be associated with the powers of creation and wisdom.

Völva - A female seer or prophetess in Norse Paganism, often associated with the practice of Seiðr.

Yggdrasil - The world tree in Norse mythology and Paganism, believed to connect the different realms of existence and sustain the natural order.

Yule - A winter solstice celebration in Norse Paganism involving feasting, gift-giving, and burning a Yule log.

Conclusion

As you near the end of this book, try to reflect back on the rich cultural heritage of the Nordic peoples and their deep reverence for the natural world. This ancient tradition, steeped in mythology and symbolism, offers a wealth of wisdom and inspiration for those seeking to connect with their ancestral roots and find meaning in their lives. A quote by the renowned writer and mythologist Joseph Campbell comes to mind: "*Myths are public dreams, dreams are private myths.*" In many ways, Norse Paganism is a reflection of this idea. The myths and stories of the Norse gods and goddesses are not just ancient tales but public dreams passed down through the generations, shaping the beliefs and practices of countless individuals over time. But, at the same time, the practice of Norse Paganism is also a deeply personal and private experience, as each individual seeks to connect with the gods and goddesses in their own way and to find meaning and guidance in their own lives.

One of the key teachings of Norse Paganism is the importance of balance and harmony in all things. This is reflected in how the Norse gods and goddesses embody light and darkness, order and chaos, and the cycles of birth, growth, decay, and rebirth inherent in the natural world. As you reflect on these teachings, you'll find inspiration to bring balance and harmony into your own life. Whether it's through meditation and mindfulness, cultivating healthy relationships and habits, or pursuing creative expression and personal growth, there are many ways to align yourself with the natural rhythms of the world around you.

At the same time, Norse Paganism emphasizes the interconnectedness of all things. From the intricate web of relationships between the gods and goddesses to the deep connections between humans and the natural world, people are part of a larger whole. In this spirit of interconnectedness, you should seek to cultivate compassion, empathy, and a sense of responsibility for the world around you. Whether it's through environmental activism, community service, or simply being kind to those around you, you can positively impact the world and contribute to the well-being of your fellow beings.

The study of Norse Paganism offers a fascinating glimpse into the rich cultural heritage of the Nordic peoples and their deep reverence for the natural world. This ancient tradition provides you with a wealth of wisdom. So, may the wisdom and teachings of Norse Paganism guide you on your journey of self-discovery and connection with the natural world. May you find balance and harmony in all aspects of your life and cultivate a sense of interconnectedness and compassion that extends beyond yourself to the world around you!

Here's another book by Mari Silva that you might like

Your Free Gift
(only available for a limited time)

Thanks for getting this book! If you want to learn more about various spirituality topics, then join Mari Silva's community and get a free guided meditation MP3 for awakening your third eye. This guided meditation mp3 is designed to open and strengthen ones third eye so you can experience a higher state of consciousness. Simply visit the link below the image to get started.

https://spiritualityspot.com/meditation

Or, Scan the QR code!

References

'Celtic' reconstructionism? (n.d.). Tairis.co.uk.

5 obscure pagan festivals around the world. (n.d.). Lonely Planet. https://www.lonelyplanet.com/articles/obscure-pagan-festivals-around-the-world

6 pagan festivals we still celebrate today. (n.d.). Sky HISTORY TV Channel. https://www.history.co.uk/articles/6-pagan-festivals-we-still-celebrate-today

Aburrow, Y. (2015, May 20). Paganism for Beginners – Overview. Dowsing for Divinity. https://www.patheos.com/blogs/sermonsfromthemound/2015/05/paganism-for-beginners1/

Adhikari, S. (2017, November 22). Top 10 important events of Ancient Greece. Ancient History Lists. https://www.ancienthistorylists.com/greek-history/top-10-important-events-of-ancient-greece/

Aldhouse-Green, M. (2015, March 13). The Celtic myths: A guide to the ancient gods and legends. Irish Times. https://www.irishtimes.com/culture/books/the-celtic-myths-a-guide-to-the-ancient-gods-and-legends-1.2136919

Annwfn –. (n.d.). British Fairies. https://britishfairies.wordpress.com/tag/annwfn/

Ásatrú. (2011, April 30). Religion Stylebook. https://religionstylebook.com/entries/asatru

BBC - wales - education - Iron Age Celts - factfile. (n.d.). BBC. https://www.bbc.co.uk/wales/celts/factfile/religion.shtml

Bealtaine rituals to celebrate the May festival. (2021, May 1). Hilda Carroll Holistic Interiors. https://www.hildacarroll.com/bealtaine-beltane/

Being Pagan; Being of the Land: Ecospirituality and Earth-Based Activities among Contemporary Pagans: Weave of reverence: Ritualizing Ecological Practice at Pagan Nature Sanctuaries. (n.d.). Harvard.edu.

https://hds.harvard.edu/publications/being-pagan-being-land-ecospirituality-and-earth-based-activities-among-0

Beltane. (2015, August 12). By Land, Sea and Sky. https://thenewpagan.wordpress.com/beltane/

Berry, L. A. (2023, March 15). Who were the Druids? A history of Druidism in Britain. British Heritage. https://britishheritage.com/history/history-druids-britain

Broome, R. (2015, October 30). The story of Ceridwen. Ceridwencentre.co.uk; Ceridwen Centre. https://ceridwencentre.co.uk/the-story-of-ceridwen/

Cartwright, M. (2021a). Ancient Celtic religion. World History Encyclopedia. https://www.worldhistory.org/Ancient_Celtic_Religion/

Cartwright, M. (2021b). Lugh. World History Encyclopedia. https://www.worldhistory.org/Lugh/

Celtic gods. (n.d.). Mythopedia. https://mythopedia.com/topics/celtic-gods

Celtic religion - The Celtic gods. (n.d.). In Encyclopedia Britannica.

Celtic religion. (2022, July 3). Roman Britain. https://www.roman-britain.co.uk/the-celts-and-celtic-life/celtic-religion/

Clan of the entangled thicket 1734. (n.d.). Blogspot.com. http://clanoftheentangledthicket.blogspot.com/2015/12/the-prediu-annwn-exploration.html

Cody. (2011, December 17). What is paganism? Pagan Federation International. https://www.paganfederation.org/what-is-paganism/

Colagrossi, M. (2018, November 27). 10 of the greatest ancient and pagan holidays. Big Think. https://bigthink.com/the-past/pagan-holidays/

Colcombe, R. (2013, July 24). The evolution of the Cauldron into a grail in Celtic Mythology. I. M. H. O. https://medium.com/i-m-h-o/the-evolution-of-the-cauldron-into-a-grail-in-celtic-mythology-a96a41604e9f

Cove, C. (2018, February 21). The whole interesting history of the Tuatha de Danann: Ireland's most ancient race. ConnollyCove. https://www.connollycove.com/tuatha-de-danann/

Dagda. (n.d.). Mythopedia. https://mythopedia.com/topics/dagda

Duffy, K. (2000). Who were the Celts? Barnes & Noble.

Eilenstein, H. (2018). Cernunnos: Vom Schamanen zum Druiden Merlin. Books on Demand.

Festivals and celebrations - RE:ONLINE. (2019, April 18). RE:ONLINE. https://www.reonline.org.uk/knowledge/paganism/festivals-and-celebrations/

Festivals and celebrations - RE:ONLINE. (2019, April 18). RE:ONLINE. https://www.reonline.org.uk/knowledge/paganism/festivals-and-celebrations/

Fields, K. (2018, October 14). Daily Pagan Rituals: List of 30+ SIMPLE Everyday Traditions. Otherworldly Oracle. https://otherworldlyoracle.com/simple-daily-pagan-rituals/

Germanic paganism. (n.d.). Religion Wiki. https://religion.fandom.com/wiki/Germanic_paganism

Germanic religion and mythology - Mythology. (n.d.). In Encyclopedia Britannica

Hart, A. (n.d.). How To Find Your Patron Deity & If You Should Even Bother. The Traveling Witch. https://thetravelingwitch.com/blog/how-to-find-your-patron-deity-if-you-should-even-bother

Hellenism. (n.d.). Paganfed.org. https://www.paganfed.org/hellenism/

Hemingway, C. (1 C.E., January 1). Greek gods and religious practices. The Met's Heilbrunn Timeline of Art History. https://www.metmuseum.org/toah/hd/grlg/hd_grlg.htm

How can I find and connect with others pagans, wiccans, and witches in my area? (n.d.). Quora. https://www.quora.com/How-can-I-find-and-connect-with-others-pagans-wiccans-and-witches-in-my-area

Jarus, O. (2022, September 23). The mysterious history of druids, ancient "mediators between humans and the gods." Livescience.com; Live Science. https://www.livescience.com/who-were-the-druids

JustCode. (n.d.). Creidhne - God of Metalworkers. - Irish God. Thewhitegoddess.co.uk. http://www.thewhitegoddess.co.uk/divinity_of_the_day/irish/creidhne.asp

King Arthur the voyager - by Katherine Langrish. (n.d.). Blogspot.com. http://the-history-girls.blogspot.com/2014/12/king-arthur-voyager-by-katherine.html

Langrish, K. (2016). Seven Miles of steel thistles: Essays on fairy tales. Greystones Press.

Litha / Midsummer. (2015, August 9). By Land, Sea and Sky. https://thenewpagan.wordpress.com/midsummer-litha/

Lugh. (n.d.). Mythopedia. https://mythopedia.com/topics/lugh

Lughnasadh / Lammas. (2015, August 9). By Land, Sea and Sky. https://thenewpagan.wordpress.com/lughnasadh-lammas/

Mabon / autumn equinox. (2015, September 3). By Land, Sea and Sky. https://thenewpagan.wordpress.com/wheel-of-the-year/mabon-autumn-equinox/

McLean, A. P. J. (n.d.). The Germanic Tribes. Lumenlearning.Com. https://courses.lumenlearning.com/atd-herkimer-westerncivilization/chapter/the-germanic-tribes/

Meet the Slavs. (2020, November 7). Slavic Magic: Rituals, Spells, and Herbs. Meet the Slavs. https://meettheslavs.com/slavic-magic/

Meet the Slavs. (2021, July 13). Slavic Paganism: History and Rituals. Meet the Slavs. https://meettheslavs.com/slavic-paganism/

Meet the Slavs. (2021, July 5). Top 6 Slavic Pagan Holidays. Meet the Slavs. https://meettheslavs.com/slavic-pagan-holidays/

My hellenismos 101. (n.d.). Hellenion.org. https://www.hellenion.org/essays-on-hellenic-polytheism/my-hellenismos-101/

Neal, C. F. (2015). Imbolc: Rituals, recipes and lore for Brigid's day. Llewellyn Publications.

No title. (n.d.-a). Study.com. https://study.com/academy/lesson/celtic-paganism-history-deities-facts-ancient-religion.html

No title. (n.d.-b). Study.com. https://study.com/learn/lesson/pantheism-religions-and-beliefs.html

O'Hara, K. (2023, January 2). The Morrigan: The story of the fiercest goddess in Irish myth. The Irish Road Trip. https://www.theirishroadtrip.com/the-morrigan/

Oertel, K. (Ed.). (2015). Ásatrú: Die Rückkehr der Götter (3rd ed.). Edition Roter Drache.

Ostara / spring equinox. (2015, August 16). By Land, Sea and Sky. https://thenewpagan.wordpress.com/ostara-spring-equinox/

Rajchel, D. (2015). Samhain: Rituals, Recipes & Lore for Halloween. Llewellyn Publications. https://thenewpagan.wordpress.com/wheel-of-the-year/samhain/

Rune, S. (2015). Paganism: The ultimate guide to paganism, inlcuding Wicca, spirituality, spells & practises for a pagan life. Createspace Independent Publishing Platform.

Sacred texts: Wicca and Neo-Paganism. (n.d.). Sacred-texts.com. https://www.sacred-texts.com/pag/

slife. (2020, June 10). Germanic Paganism. The Spiritual Life. https://slife.org/germanic-paganism/

Smith, D. (2016, March 26). Wiccan holidays: Celebrating the sun on the Sabbats. Dummies. https://www.dummies.com/article/body-mind-spirit/religion-spirituality/wicca/wiccan-holidays-celebrating-the-sun-on-the-sabbats-192774/

Sunshine, G. (2020, February 4). Wicca and eclectic Neo-Paganism: Beliefs and practices, emerging worldviews 22. Breakpoint. https://breakpoint.org/wicca-and-eclectic-neo-paganism-beliefs-and-practices-emerging-worldviews-22/

The Absolute Basics Paganism. (n.d.). Umass.edu. https://www.umass.edu/rso/spirals/Site/Paganism_101.html

The Current Chief, The Former Chief, & Patroness, O. (2019a, November 27). Druid beliefs. Order of Bards, Ovates & Druids; OBOD. https://druidry.org/druid-way/beliefs

The Current Chief, The Former Chief, & Patroness, O. (2019b, November 27). History of the druids. Order of Bards, Ovates & Druids; OBOD. https://druidry.org/druid-way/what-druidry/a-longer-history

The Hellenistic period-cultural & historical overview. (2018, June 14). Department of Classics. https://www.colorado.edu/classics/2018/06/14/hellenistic-period-cultural-historical-overview

The old Nordic religion today. (n.d.). National Museum of Denmark. https://en.natmus.dk/historical-knowledge/denmark/prehistoric-period-until-1050-ad/the-viking-age/religion-magic-death-and-rituals/the-old-nordic-religion-today/

The Pagan year. (n.d.). BBC. https://www.bbc.co.uk/religion/religions/paganism/holydays/year.shtml

The Witch is In. (n.d.). Tumblr. https://herecomesthewitch.tumblr.com/post/157912148899/laurels-guide-to-grimoires

The. (2018, August 10). Neo-paganism offers something old and something new. Economist (London, England: 1843). https://www.economist.com/erasmus/2018/08/10/neo-paganism-offers-something-old-and-something-new

Thomas, P. V. (n.d.). Ancient Celtic Religion. Tutorialspoint.com. https://www.tutorialspoint.com/ancient-celtic-religion

V. (2018). Morrigan. Independently Published.

What is Asatru? (2013, December 4). Gotquestions.org. https://www.gotquestions.org/Asatru.html

Wheel of the Year. (2013, June 22). The Celtic Journey. https://thecelticjourney.wordpress.com/the-celts/wheel-of-the-year/

Wheel of the Year: The 8 Wiccan holiday festivals - Wicca Academy. (n.d.). https://wiccaacademy.com/wheel-of-the-year/

Who were the Druids? (2017, March 21). Historic UK. https://www.historic-uk.com/HistoryUK/HistoryofWales/Druids/

Wigington, P. (2007, August 19). Hellenic Polytheism and the Reconstruction of Greek Paganism. Learn Religions. https://www.learnreligions.com/about-hellenic-polytheism-2562548

Wigington, P. (2007a, June 24). The legend of Lugh, the Celtic craftsman god. Learn Religions. https://www.learnreligions.com/lugh-master-of-skills-2561970

Wigington, P. (2007b, September 19). Brighid, the hearth goddess of Ireland. Learn Religions. https://www.learnreligions.com/brighid-hearth-goddess-of-ireland-2561958

Wigington, P. (2008a, November 2). The Morrighan. Learn Religions. https://www.learnreligions.com/the-morrighan-of-ireland-2561971

Wigington, P. (2008b, December 13). Cernunnos, the wild Celtic god of the Forest. Learn Religions. https://www.learnreligions.com/cernunnos-wild-god-of-the-forest-2561959

Wigington, P. (2009, August 7). Pagan gods and goddesses. Learn Religions. https://www.learnreligions.com/pagan-gods-and-goddesses-2561985

Wigington, P. (2009a, August 4). The Dagda, the father god of Ireland. Learn Religions. https://www.learnreligions.com/the-dagda-father-god-of-ireland-2561706

Wigington, P. (2009b, August 5). 10 Celtic deities you should know. Learn Religions. https://www.learnreligions.com/gods-of-the-celts-2561711

Wigington, P. (2012, June 20). Resources for Celtic pagans. Learn Religions. https://www.learnreligions.com/resources-for-celtic-pagans-2562555

Wigington, P. (n.d.). The 10 Most Important Slavic Gods. ThoughtCo. https://www.thoughtco.com/slavic-gods-4768505

wikiHow. (2011, July 30). How to Set up a Simple Pagan or Wiccan Altar. WikiHow. https://www.wikihow.com/Set-up-a-Simple-Pagan-or-Wiccan-Altar

Wright, M. S. (2013, January 23). Ideas for Celebrating Pagan Holidays With Family and Children. Exemplore. https://exemplore.com/paganism/Imbolc-for-Pagan-Families-Ideas-for-Celebrating-with-Children

Yule / Midwinter. (2015, August 27). By Land, Sea and Sky. https://thenewpagan.wordpress.com/wheel-of-the-year/yule-midwinter/

ztevetevans. (2021, April 30). Celtic lore: Cauldrons – the magical, the mythical and the real. Under the Influence! https://ztevetevans.wordpress.com/2021/04/30/celtic-lore-cauldrons-the-magical-the-mythical-and-the-real

6 types of spirit guides & how to communicate with them. (2015, January 23). Mindbodygreen. https://www.mindbodygreen.com/articles/types-of-spirit-guides

Aburrow, Y. (n.d.). utiseta –. Dowsing for Divinity. https://dowsingfordivinity.com/tag/utiseta/

Aletheia. (2016, March 10). Scrying: How to practice the ancient art of second sight (with pictures). LonerWolf. https://lonerwolf.com/scrying/

Aletheia. (2018, February 5). 7 types of spirit guides (& how to connect with them). LonerWolf. https://lonerwolf.com/spirit-guides/

Ancient Roots, Historical Challenges. (n.d.). Pluralism.Org. https://pluralism.org/ancient-roots-historical-challenges

Anne C. Sørensen, R. M. J. H. (n.d.). Runes. Vikingeskibsmuseet i Roskilde.

https://www.vikingeskibsmuseet.dk/en/professions/education/viking-age-people/runes

Ásatrú Definitions for Journalists. (n.d.). Norsemyth.org. https://www.norsemyth.org/2013/09/asatru-definition-for-journalists.html

Asatru Holidays. (n.d.). Thetroth.org. https://thetroth.org/resources/norse-pagan-holidays

Athar, K., Fey, T., Mabanta, D., Brian, P., Jackson, L., Damian, D. D., Scheucher, A., Paler, J., & Brown, J. (2020, August 21). What is shamanic breathwork and how is it used? Ideapod. https://ideapod.com/shamanic-breathwork/

Brethauer, A. (2021, September 10). Bind runes discover their simple and powerful Norse magic. The Peculiar Brunette; Amanda Brethauer. https://www.thepeculiarbrunette.com/bind-runes/

Byatt, A. S. (2011). Ragnarok: The end of the gods. Canongate Books. https://norse-mythology.org/tales/ragnarok/

Campbell, H. (2020, February 15). What is asatru? VikingStyle. https://viking-styles.com/blogs/history/what-is-asatru

Chambers, J. (2019, December 7). Ásatrú - Iceland's fastest growing non-Christian religion. All Things Iceland. https://allthingsiceland.com/asatru-icelands-fastest-growing-non-christian-religion/

Chris. (2022, July 2). A Complete Guide to Norse Gods & Goddesses. Panorama. https://panoramaglasslodge.com/a-complete-guide-to-norse-gods-goddesses/

Christianity.com Editorial Staff. (2019, September 23). Who Are Pagans? The History and Beliefs of Paganism. Christianity.Com. https://www.christianity.com/wiki/cults-and-other-religions/pagans-history-and-beliefs-of-paganism.html

Dan. (2012, November 15). Seidr. Norse Mythology for Smart People. https://norse-mythology.org/concepts/seidr/

Death & the afterlife. (2021, October 25). Skald's Keep. https://skaldskeep.com/norse/norse-afterlife/

Death and the Afterlife. (2012, November 15). Norse Mythology for Smart People. https://norse-mythology.org/concepts/death-and-the-afterlife/

Death and the Afterlife. (2012, November 15). Norse Mythology for Smart People. https://norse-mythology.org/concepts/death-and-the-afterlife/

Eliade, M., & Diószegi, V. (2022). shamanism. In Encyclopedia Britannica.

Estrada, J. (2020, March 11). How to use oracle cards, the simpler-to-read cousin of tarot that helps you tap into your intuition. Well+Good. https://www.wellandgood.com/how-to-use-oracle-cards/

Fields, K. (2021, December 29). Norse Magic: Seidr, Shapeshifting, Runes, & More. Otherworldly Oracle. https://otherworldlyoracle.com/norse-magic/

Folkvang. (2016, July 6). Norse Mythology for Smart People. https://norse-mythology.org/folkvang/

Glossary of Frequently Recurring Terms and names. (2012, March 1). Romantic-circles.org. https://romantic-circles.org/editions/norse/HTML/Glossary.html

Greenberg, M. (2020, November 16). Seidr magic in viking culture. MythologySource; Mike Greenberg, PhD. https://mythologysource.com/seidr-magic-viking-culture/

Gregg. (2010, May 23). How To Take a Shamanic Journey. Warrior Mind Coach. https://www.warriormindcoach.com/how-to-take-a-shamanic-journey/

Groeneveld, E. (2017). Norse mythology. World History Encyclopedia. https://www.worldhistory.org/Norse_Mythology/

Hel (goddess). (2012, November 15). Norse Mythology for Smart People. https://norse-mythology.org/gods-and-creatures/giants/hel/

Hel (The Underworld). (2012, November 15). Norse Mythology for Smart People. https://norse-mythology.org/cosmology/the-nine-worlds/helheim/

Helms, M. F. (2012). Valhalla. Createspace Independent Publishing Platform.

History of modern Paganism. (n.d.). https://www.bbc.co.uk/religion/religions/paganism/history/modern_1.shtml

How to consecrate runes. (2012, October 22). Allegheny Candles' Blog. https://alleghenycandles.wordpress.com/2012/10/22/how-to-consecrate-runes/

Jessica, S. (2019, June 3). Norse mythology afterlife. Norse and Viking Mythology; vkngjewelry. https://blog.vkngjewelry.com/en/norse-afterlife/

Lachlan, M. D. (2011). Fenrir. Prometheus Books.

Mrs, B. (2020, August 13). Intro to bindrunes. LunaOwl. https://luna-owl.com/2020/08/13/intro-to-bindrunes/

Nikel, D. (2019, August 21). Viking Religion: From the Norse Gods to Christianity. Life in Norway. https://www.lifeinnorway.net/viking-religion/

Nine Realms. (n.d.). Mythopedia. https://mythopedia.com/topics/nine-realms

Nomads, T. (2019, December 1). How to Make Your Own Rune Set. Time Nomads | Your Pagan Store Online. https://www.timenomads.com/how-to-make-your-own-rune-set/

Nomads, T. (2020, October 8). Rune Magic 101: What are and How to Make Bind Runes. Time Nomads | Your Pagan Store Online. https://www.timenomads.com/rune-magic-101-what-are-and-how-to-make-norse-bind-runes/

Nordic Wiccan. (n.d.). Blogspot.com. http://nordicwiccan.blogspot.com/p/httpnordicwiccanblogspotcom201404glossa.html

Nordic Wiccan. (n.d.-a). Blogspot.com. http://nordicwiccan.blogspot.com/2014/06/rune-yoga.html

Nordic Wiccan. (n.d.-b). Blogspot.com. http://nordicwiccan.blogspot.com/2013/07/runic-yoga.html

Norse pagan definitions. (2020, May 15). Skald's Keep. https://skaldskeep.com/terms-defined/

Northern Tradition Paganism: What is Rökkatru? (n.d.). Northernpaganism.Org. https://www.northernpaganism.org/rokkatru/what-is-rokkatru.html

Northern Tradition Shamanism: Utiseta, Breath, and Mound-Sitting. (n.d.). Northernshamanism.Org. http://www.northernshamanism.org/utiseta-breath-and-mound-sitting.html

Oddities, O. (2019, April 24). How to make a bindrune. Oreamnos Oddities. https://oreamnosoddities.com/blogs/news/how-to-make-a-bindrune

Oertel, K. (Ed.). (2015). Ásatrú: Die Rückkehr der Götter (3rd ed.). Edition Roter Drache.

Pagan beliefs. (n.d.). https://www.bbc.co.uk/religion/religions/paganism/beliefs/beliefs.shtml

Pat. (2020, December 8). The viking self and its parts. Maier Files Series. https://www.maier-files.com/the-viking-self-and-its-parts/

Pat. (2020, December 8). The viking self and its parts. Maier Files Series. https://www.maier-files.com/the-viking-self-and-its-parts/

Rode, B. (2021, April 13). Meet your spirit guide. Phoebe Garnsworthy. https://www.phoebegarnsworthy.com/meet-your-spirit-guide/

Runer og magi. (n.d.). Avaldsnes. https://avaldsnes.info/en/viking/lorem-ipsum/

Runes. (2012, November 14). Norse Mythology for Smart People. https://norse-mythology.org/runes/

Runes. (2021, October 26). Skald's Keep. https://skaldskeep.com/norse/runes/

Runic Philosophy and Magic. (2013, June 29). Norse Mythology for Smart People. https://norse-mythology.org/runes/runic-philosophy-and-magic/

SACRED CALENDER of ASATRU. (n.d.). Odinsvolk.Ca. http://odinsvolk.ca/O.V.A.%20-%20SACRED%20CALENDER.htm

Sam, T. +., & Wander, T. (2020, November 25). Rune Meanings And How To Use Rune Stones For Divination —. Two Wander x Elysium Rituals. https://www.twowander.com/blog/rune-meanings-how-to-use-runestones-for-divination

Sarenth, /. (2011, February 1). Stadhagaldr and breathing the Runes. Sarenth Odinsson. https://sarenth.wordpress.com/2011/02/01/stadhagaldr-and-breathing-the-runes/

Sebastiani, A. (2020). Paganism for beginners: The complete guide to nature-based spirituality for every new seeker. Rockridge Press.

Seidr Cleansing Ritual. (n.d.). Heathen Designs. https://www.heathenbydesign.com/seidr-cleansing-ritual

Shamanism. (2012, November 15). Norse Mythology for Smart People. https://norse-mythology.org/concepts/shamanism/

Shelley, A. (2023, January 9). Futhark Runes: Symbols, Meanings and How to Use Them. Andrea Shelley Designs. https://andreashelley.com/blog/futhark-runes-symbols-and-meanings/

shirleytwofeathers. (n.d.). Runic postures. Shirleytwofeathers.com. https://shirleytwofeathers.com/The_Blog/magickal-ingredients/runic-postures/

Sister, W. (2016, July 19). How to work with your spirit animal: A total guide. The Numinous. https://www.the-numinous.com/2016/07/19/work-with-your-spirit-animal/

Skjalden. (2018, March 11). Völva the viking witch or seeress. Nordic Culture. https://skjalden.com/volva-the-viking-witch-or-seeress/

Stàdhagaldr. (n.d.). Blogspot.com. http://galdrtanz-runedance.blogspot.com/2013/03/stadhagaldr.html

Strmiska, M. (2000). Ásatrú in Iceland: The rebirth of Nordic Paganism? Nova Religio The Journal of Alternative and Emergent Religions, 4(1), 106–132. https://doi.org/10.1525/nr.2000.4.1.106

Tetrault, S., & BA. (2020, March 29). What's the Norse, or Viking, afterlife supposed to be like? Joincake.com. https://www.joincake.com/blog/norse-afterlife/

The Meanings of the Runes. (2013, June 29). Norse Mythology for Smart People. https://norse-mythology.org/runes/the-meanings-of-the-runes/

The multi-part soul. (2021, October 27). Skald's Keep. https://skaldskeep.com/norse/soul/

The old Nordic religion today. (n.d.). National Museum of Denmark. https://en.natmus.dk/historical-knowledge/denmark/prehistoric-period-until-1050-ad/the-viking-age/religion-magic-death-and-rituals/the-old-nordic-religion-today/

The Origins of the Runes. (2013, June 29). Norse Mythology for Smart People. https://norse-mythology.org/runes/the-origins-of-the-runes/

The Self and Its Parts. (2012, November 15). Norse Mythology for Smart People. https://norse-mythology.org/concepts/the-parts-of-the-self/

The Self and Its Parts. (2012, November 15). Norse Mythology for Smart People. https://norse-mythology.org/concepts/the-parts-of-the-self/

Time Nomads. (2020, October 8). Rune magic 101: What are and how to make bind runes. Time Nomads | Your Pagan Store Online; Time Nomads. https://www.timenomads.com/rune-magic-101-what-are-and-how-to-make-norse-bind-runes/

Unrau, B. (2008). Scrying. CaltexPress.

Útiseta: The Norse Shaman's Wilderness Quest. (n.d.). Shanegadd.Com. https://www.shanegadd.com/post/útiseta-the-norse-shaman-s-wilderness-quest

Valhalla. (n.d.). Mythopedia. https://mythopedia.com/topics/valhalla

Vanatru. (n.d.). WikiPagan. https://pagan.fandom.com/wiki/Vanatru

What Do Pagans Do? (n.d.). Pluralism.Org. https://pluralism.org/what-do-pagans-do

What is deep meditation? Techniques & experiences. (2017, August 28). Mindworks Meditation. https://mindworks.org/blog/what-is-deep-meditation/

What were the similarities and differences between Anglo Saxon Paganism and Norse Paganism? (n.d.). Quora. https://www.quora.com/What-were-the-similarities-and-differences-between-Anglo-Saxon-Paganism-and-Norse-Paganism

White, E. D. (2023). Paganism. In Encyclopedia Britannica.

Who were the Viking Gods? (n.d.). Twinkl. https://www.twinkl.co.uk/teaching-wiki/viking-gods

Wigington, P. (2007, June 28). Asatru - Norse heathens of modern Paganism. Learn Religions. https://www.learnreligions.com/asatru-modern-paganism-2562545

Wigington, P. (2012, June 5). The Nine Noble Virtues of Asatru. Learn Religions. https://www.learnreligions.com/noble-virtues-of-asatru-2561539

Yggdrasil. (n.d.). Mythopedia. https://mythopedia.com/topics/yggdrasil

Yugay, I. (2018, January 15). Deep meditation – connection with your soul. Mindvalley Blog. https://blog.mindvalley.com/deep-meditation/

Yule. (n.d.). Thetroth.org. https://thetroth.org/resources/holidays/yule

Image Sources

[1] https://pixabay.com/images/id-6982525/

[2] https://unsplash.com/photos/KnBHXJzqIRs?utm_source=unsplash&utm_medium=referral&utm_content=creditShareLink

[3] https://commons.wikimedia.org/wiki/File:Edda.jpg

[4] https://commons.wikimedia.org/wiki/File:Olaus_Magnus_-_On_the_Geats%27_Worship_and_Sacrifice.jpg

[5] Mhapon, CC BY-SA 4.0 <https://creativecommons.org/licenses/by-sa/4.0>, via Wikimedia Commons: https://commons.wikimedia.org/wiki/File:Dadzbog.jpg

[6] Immortality113, CC BY-SA 4.0 <https://creativecommons.org/licenses/by-sa/4.0>, via Wikimedia Commons: https://commons.wikimedia.org/wiki/File:Mt-olympus_gods.jpg

[7] https://unsplash.com/photos/-A[RBlhuaHE?utm_source=unsplash&utm_medium=referral&utm_content=creditShareLink

[8] https://unsplash.com/photos/OfaDD5o8hpk?utm_source=unsplash&utm_medium=referral&utm_content=creditShareLink

[9] https://unsplash.com/photos/-G3rw6Y02D0?utm_source=unsplash&utm_medium=referral&utm_content=creditShareLink

[10] https://commons.wikimedia.org/wiki/File:Odin_(Manual_of_Mythology).jpg

[11] Et2brute, CC0, via Wikimedia Commons: https://commons.wikimedia.org/wiki/File:Nine_Realms.svg

[12] Photograph by Jónína K. Berg, CC BY-SA 3.0 <https://creativecommons.org/licenses/by-sa/3.0>, via Wikimedia Commons: https://commons.wikimedia.org/wiki/File:Sveinbj%C3%B6rn_Beinteinsson_1991.jpg

[13] Oluf Bagge, Public domain, via Wikimedia Commons: https://commons.wikimedia.org/wiki/File:Oluf_Olufsen_Bagge_-

_Yggdrasil,_The_Mundane_Tree_1847_-_full_page.jpg

[14] *Emil Doepler, Public domain, via Wikimedia Commons:*
https://commons.wikimedia.org/wiki/File:Walhall_by_Emil_Doepler.jpg

[15] https://unsplash.com/photos/ie8WW5KUx3o?utm_source=unsplash&utm_medium=referral&utm_content=creditShareLink

[16] https://unsplash.com/photos/ZOxkaXFvw6A?utm_source=unsplash&utm_medium=referral&utm_content=creditShareLink

[17] https://www.pexels.com/photo/white-and-brown-ceramic-bowl-1793035/

[18] https://www.pexels.com/photo/silhouette-of-person-raising-its-hand-268134/

[19] *Pious Shy Boi, CC0, via Wikimedia Commons:*
https://commons.wikimedia.org/wiki/File:Runic_Square_Font.png

[20] https://commons.wikimedia.org/wiki/File:Ing_bindrune.png

www.ingramcontent.com/pod-product-compliance
Lightning Source LLC
Chambersburg PA
CBHW051853160426
43209CB00006B/1288